Passport
to English

**MACMILLAN
CAMEROON**

© Copyright text Ron Holt 2001
© Copyright illustrations Macmillan Education 2001

All rights reserved. No reproduction, copy or transmission of this publication may be made without written permission.

No paragraph of this publication may be reproduced, copied or transmitted save with written permission or in accordance with the provisions of the Copyright, Designs and Patents Act 1988, or under the terms of any licence permitting limited copying issued by the Copyright Licensing Agency, 90 Tottenham Court Road, London W1P 9HE.

Any person who does any unauthorised act in relation to this publication may be liable to criminal prosecution and civil claims for damages.

First published 2001 by
MACMILLAN CAMEROON LTD
P.O. Box 1028
Limbe
Republic of Cameroon

ISBN 9956–12–015–4

10 9   8   7   6   5   4   3   2   1
10 09 08 07 06 05 04 03 02 01

This book is printed on paper suitable for recycling and made from fully managed and sustained forest sources.

Typeset by EXPO Holdings, Malaysia

Printed in Malaysia

A catalogue record for this book is available from the British Library

Contents

1 Introduction   1

  1.1 Features and aims   1
  1.2 Syllabus and course design   2
  1.3 Quantity and sequence of material   2
  1.4 Methodology   3
  1.5 Organising closed pairwork   3
  1.6 Correction and marking   4
  1.7 The place of grammar   5
  1.8 Passive and active vocabulary   6
  1.9 Revision   6
  1.10 Evaluation   7

2 General teaching procedures   8

  2.1 Developing vocabulary   8
  2.2 Introducing topics   9
  2.3 Focus on reading   9
  2.4 Focus on speaking   10
  2.5 Focus on listening   11
  2.6 Focus on pronunciation   12
  2.7 Focus on writing   12
  2.8 Integrating literature   13

3 Unit-by-unit teaching notes   14

  Unit 1   14
  Unit 2   16
  Unit 3   20
  Unit 4   22
  Unit 5   24
  Unit 6   28
  Unit 7   31
  Unit 8   33
  Unit 9   36
  Unit 10   39

iv CONTENTS

Unit 11	43
Unit 12	45
Unit 13	48
Unit 14	49
Unit 15	51
Appendix 1 Contents analysis table	56
Appendix 2 Listening comprehension texts	63
Appendix 3 Wordlist	70

1 Introduction

1.1 Features and aims

***Passport to English* Student's Book 5** is a continuation of Book 4 and is for students in Year 5 of Senior Secondary School. It builds on the foundations of previous levels, helping teachers to continue introducing modern ideas about English language teaching and learning in a practical way.

The course continues to focus on:
- regular active, communicative use of English by the students, rather than merely teaching them about the language;
- purposeful lessons (helping students to understand what they are doing and why; choosing content which students will feel is relevant to them);
- development of students' intellectual abilities, by ensuring that language practice is not merely mechanical, but contains a degree of mental challenge. Students are often expected to perform a personal judgement on the basis of information given, or to express an opinion based on their own personal experience;
- understanding of the different ways in which English is used as a medium of communication in the student's own country, and as an international language in the rest of the world;
- help with the learning of other subjects in the curriculum through the medium of English. In this connection, a sensible balance is struck between the duty of English teachers to service the teaching of other subjects, and their prime responsibilities, which are for developing language for purposes of communication, creativity and personal development.

Passport to English follows an integrated approach, in which there is an interaction between:
- the development of vocabulary;
- the teaching of grammatical structures and patterns and ways in which English functions;
- practice in the principal language skills (reading comprehension, listening comprehension, spoken English and writing), including sub-skills which support them, such as punctuation and pronunciation.

2 INTRODUCTION

In **Passport to English**, the approach to grammar and structures is both remedial and developmental. A special feature is the **Grammar Review Section** which appears at the back of the **Student's Book**, and complementary study notes in the individual units of the **Student's Book**.

The **Student's Book** also contains another section at the back of the book, which is devoted to vocabulary development. This is in the form of a magazine called WORD.

1.2 Syllabus and course design

Passport to English 5 is tailor-made to provide substantial practice in the Cameroon GCE O-level English Language requirements. It systematically identifies and deals with the sub-skills of Directed Writing and Understanding and Response, as well as Listening Comprehension. In the **Contents analysis table** (**Appendix 1** at the back of this book) teachers can find out what they will be teaching during a particular unit, and also how this fits into the official syllabus. The contents page in the **Student's Book** also provides a useful summary.

All learning activities in **Passport to English** are organised around a number of topics which are relevant to the needs and interests of students at the Senior Secondary level. Each topic is studied from a number of different angles, in several consecutive units of the book.

The main topics of the book are:
- family life;
- social conditions and attitudes;
- empowerment of women;
- science and education;
- crime;
- ecology and health.

These topics are not treated in isolation, but linked together. Furthermore, opportunities are also taken to link all topics to the themes of man's use of and responsibility for the natural environment in which the human race lives, the individual's role in society, and society's responsibilities towards the individual.

1.3 Quantity and sequence of material

The course is divided into 15 Units, with a **Practice Test** inserted after every fifth unit. Each Unit provides a range of activities which, in an average class, is sufficient for up to two weeks' work. The course is therefore intended to provide a complete programme of language and integrated literature which will normally occupy most of the teaching time that is available to you.

Some of the work in the **Student's Book** is suitable for homework, and if this is so, it is normally indicated in the **Unit-by-Unit notes**.

Units have been planned so that students will feel there is variety in the work, and early activities in a unit often prepare for later ones. For these reasons, you should consider carefully before changing the sequence of activities.

1.4 *Methodology*

Passport to English is a course in which the principal language skills (listening, speaking, reading and writing) are developed in an integrated way. We take the view that these skills reinforce each other as students acquire the language, and none of them should be neglected.

As students move closer to more academic study, and as their ability to appreciate and gain from literature also grows, it is natural that reading texts should be the main vehicle for presenting new language. The texts are mainly extracts from contemporary newspapers and magazines, but also include public and personal correspondence. The topics – and hence new language – are presented through the texts, some of which are the work of African authors of distinction. Adaptation, simplification and shortening of original texts is kept to a minimum, consistent with providing suitable teaching material.

The course actively promotes learner independence. Silent reading is only one of the ways in which we encourage students to be independent and accept increasing responsibility for their own progress. Another is pairwork, which is used in oral activities. By pairwork we mean equal amounts of work in open pairs (one pair practises while the rest of the class listens) followed by closed pairwork (every student in the class practises simultaneously with a partner).

1.5 *Organising closed pairwork*

Students who used ***Passport to English*** in Junior Secondary School have been trained to do pairwork, but for your own information here is an explanation of the technique they are used to.

Form pairs by giving a simple instruction, such as 'Do this exercise with your usual partner' or 'If you're in row 1, 3 or 5, talk about the picture with the students sitting behind you. That means, if you're siting in row 2, 4 or 6, you'll talk to the student sitting in front of you.'

If the class does not easily divide into pairs, you can form groups of three or four instead. (In a group of three, one student will take part A, and two will take part B. In a group of four students, there will be two students for each part.)

Teachers who have not used closed pairwork before may have some initial doubts about it. They may worry that they will not be able to hear and correct every mistake which is made; they may be concerned that some students will simply waste their time, perhaps speaking some language other than English; they may worry about their own role, and feel that they are not doing enough to teach the class; they may fear too much noise and loss of control.

These are indeed real problems, but the advantages of closed pairwork outweigh the disadvantages, because pairwork increases the amount of individual practice which each student can get, and it motivates students very strongly. It also benefits self-conscious students. (For these reasons, students are usually cooperative.) So we must look for ways round the problems. Usually they disappear if the following steps are taken.

1 Continue open pairwork until you are confident that few mistakes will be made when closed pairs are formed.
2 Walk round the class so that you can check whether mistakes are being made, and also detect any students who are not working properly. If you hear something wrong, don't immediately interrupt, but listen to hear if it happens again. Then perhaps a whispered correction in one student's ear will be enough. If you hear several pairs making the same mistake, perhaps call for the whole class's attention and give everyone an explanation; or make a note of the error, and deal with it after the pairwork activity has been completed.
3 Pairwork often involves one of the pair asking a question and the other answering it. Make sure both students in each pair have a chance to do both, by switching the roles round halfway through the exercise.
4 So that students are serious and active in closed pairwork, it should be evaluated. Tell students at the start of the year that you will be assessing their pairwork continuously, and if possible award a proportion of the final examination marks for pairwork.

1.6 Correction and marking

Correction and marking serve many purposes:
- to encourage students by giving them advice about their strengths and weaknesses;

- to identify points which you may need to revise and practise further;
- to evaluate students' performances and give them information about their standards of achievement;
- to develop students' ability to be self-critical.

When correcting written work, there is always a danger of overmarking. To avoid this, read the piece of work (whether it is a dictation, summary or composition) through to the end before you correct anything. Then decide on one (or more) types of error that you will concentrate on this time. This may be an error of structure, e.g. poor use of linking devices such as *because, so, as to, however, in spite of*; or it may be an error of style, e.g. overuse of the pronoun *I*, or too many short sentences which would be better linked together in some way. Describe the error, and give an example of how it may be corrected. Then simply underline or circle places where similar errors occur, and leave them for the students to correct by themselves.

In all written work students should be trained to write out corrections to their previous work before starting a new piece.

Whilst it is always necessary to correct written work promptly, it is not always necessary to give a mark. In fact, with longer pieces of connected writing (compositions, stories, essays) it is best to ask students to start by writing a draft. The teacher should check the draft to see if it meets the task requirements in terms of register, form, number of words and paragraphs. Correct the draft and return it without awarding a mark, but tell each student what mark you would give the piece of work in its present form, and also the mark you have in mind if the student manages to improve it in the ways you have suggested. As the student sets about rewriting the piece of work, he/she has a real incentive to improve it before handing in the final version for marking.

1.7 *The place of grammar*

Grammar teaching is concerned with rules governing the forms of the language. We cannot say exactly what we want to say, or be completely accepted in certain social situations, without observing such rules. But there is more to speaking and writing a language than knowing its rules. Students must also know about the meanings of sentences and the purposes for which they are spoken or written – that is, their functions – and they must understand that words often imply more than their strict meaning. For example, 'You're standing on my foot!' is not normally said to give someone a piece of information, but is an angry, indirect request to have the foot removed.

6 INTRODUCTION

Passport to English pays attention to both form and function. In the **Student's Book** there are sections on both. The **Grammar Review Section** covers grammar which has been covered in Junior Secondary, but which may have been imperfectly learnt and still causes problems. Revision is made more systematic by organisation into a system, progressing from parts of speech to simple sentences, and then to compound and complex sentences. The **Focus on grammar** sections in the teaching units deal mainly with extensions to the grammar learnt in Junior Secondary.

1.8 Passive and active vocabulary

Students who reach Senior Secondary already possess a sufficient vocabulary to be able to talk and write about common everyday topics. We call the vocabulary which they can call to mind and produce for talking and writing their *active vocabulary*.

There are many more words which students might not be able to recall for use in their own speech and writing, but which they recognise and understand when they come across them, either in listening or in reading. These additional words form their *passive vocabulary*.

In this course the active vocabulary is developed into more specialised areas, but the majority of new words which the students will meet fall into the passive category. This means that you should not expect the students to produce them easily in speech; but they should be able to read them comfortably and spell them, and for the purposes of writing, they should be able to find them again with the aid of their vocabulary book, or a dictionary.

Each student naturally develops a a different active and passive vocabulary of his own. As a rough guide to what may be expected, words for the active vocabulary are printed **like this** in the **Unit-by-unit teaching notes** and listed in the **Contents analysis table**. Words that are practised in vocabulary exercises are printed in colour in the **Student's Book** and listed in the **Wordlist** which appears in both the **Student's Book** and the **Teacher's Book**.

1.9 Revision

The **Grammar Review Section** is used for regular, continuous revision. In some Units, students are set certain sections to study.

They should be given the opportunity to ask questions about any points which they do not fully understand.

Study of the **Grammar Review Section** is necessary as preparation for the **Practice Tests**, and it will also be useful during final preparation before the end-of-year examination.

1.10 *Evaluation*

Practice Tests are provided after Units 5, 10 and 15 in the **Student's Book**. These are in line with the National Syllabus and focus on: Understanding and response; Directed writing; Listening comprehension; Picture composition; Essay writing.

2 General teaching procedures

2.1 Developing vocabulary

Much of the vocabulary taught during the course belongs to the topic areas outlined in **Section 1.2**. To this are added a number of words of general use which were not included in the active vocabulary of previous levels of *Passport to English*.

You can identify the 'new' words to be taught in each unit in three ways: by looking at the **Student's Book**, where they are printed in colour; by looking at the **Unit-by-unit teaching notes**, where they are printed **like this**; and by looking at the **Contents analysis table** (**Appendix 1** at the back of this book).

Most new words are presented in the main reading texts. Occasionally, it is a good idea to pre-teach some of the words printed in colour or listed in the **Unit-by-unit teaching notes**, before students read the passage. But the majority of words should not be pre-taught. Instead, students should be given the chance to guess the meanings from context. In addition, there are vocabulary exercises after passages containing words printed in colour. In addition to checking understanding of new words, the teacher should, of course, make sure that students learn their spelling and how to pronounce them correctly.

This approach to vocabulary has the advantage that students become accustomed to working out the meanings of unfamiliar words, as they may have to do in public examinations, as well as in real-life situations outside school.

In Senior Secondary School it is essential that all students have access to a good English-only learner's dictionary, such as the *Advanced Learner's Dictionary* (Oxford), the *Dictionary of Contemporary English* (Longman), or the *Macmillan Student's Dictionary*. At frequent points in the **Student's Book**, students are given practice in using extracts from two of these dictionaries, but beyond this it is up to the teacher to find suitable moments when students can make constructive use of a dictionary.

As well as a dictionary, it is assumed that students will have a vocabulary book in which they can record words they have just learnt as additions to their active vocabulary. You may wish students to write the vocabulary exercises (mentioned above) in these vocabulary books. This could be done in pencil first, and then, after correction, inked in. Such entries will be the basis of revision before spelling tests and dictations. As the topics are dealt with in blocks of units, it will happen naturally that most words for a given topic will appear as a set in the students' vocabulary books, and in this respect the vocabulary books will be usefully different from the **Wordlist**, printed at the back of the **Student's Book**, which is in alphabetical order. (This **Wordlist** can also be found in **Appendix 3** of this book.)

In addition to new words in the main units, the WORD Magazine at the back of the **Student's Book** presents additional vocabulary connected with the topics outlined in **Section 1.2**. The intention is that this additional reading and learning of words from context will be done at home. To preserve the illusion we wish to create, that students are reading a magazine, there are no comprehension questions in this vocabulary development section.

2.2 Introducing topics and tasks

Students are rational human beings, and therefore need to have a clear idea of what they are going to do, and why. For this reason it is important to introduce each new topic and task as you come to it, and to make it seem like something worth knowing more about. Both the **Unit-by-unit teaching notes** in this book and the first step of each Unit in the **Student's Book** provide some ideas for presenting new topics and tasks in a motivating way.

2.3 Focus on reading

You should decide beforehand how you want a reading passage to be read. Use four different instructions:
- *Read this together* (i.e. you or one or more of your students read aloud, while the rest of the class listen and follow in their books).
- *Read this silently* (i.e. everyone in the class reads on his own). Give this instruction for the first reading of texts.
- *Read this in the way I tell you* (This instruction is usually given when a passage is so long that you may wish different sections to be read in different ways, in order to stimulate the class with variety, e.g. you start by reading a section aloud yourself, then ask one or more students to carry on reading

aloud, then let the class read a section silently, and so on. With long texts it may also be a good idea to pause to ask a few factual check questions before moving on, especially after a section which has been read silently.)
- *Read this for pleasure* (see the notes in the last paragraph of **Section 2.8**).

Pay attention to the suggestions in the **Unit-by-unit teaching notes** about when to teach any new words in the passage (see also **Section 2.1** on this point).

Each main reading passage in an Understanding and Response Unit is followed by a section containing various types of exercises: to test comprehension, to develop vocabulary, and to encourage discussion. The comprehension section is intended to reflect the type of comprehension questions in the GCE exam. Therefore the teacher needs to indicate to students some general guidelines on how to go about doing comprehension, for example: using context clues, skimming and scanning, dictionary skills. An additional skill required is that of comparing two texts.

In Directed Writing Units, reading passages are followed by a writing task.

The various activities need not all be done in class, nor need they all be done in the same lesson. Use your discretion about this.

If there is spare time when a Unit has been completed, let students re-read a passage quickly, on their own. Then, with books closed, let them ask each other questions from memory about the passage. This may be done in closed or open pairs, and possibly organised as a team game, with a point for each good question and another point for each good answer.

2.4 Focus on speaking

Discussions

Discussions should be an important part of almost every English lesson. When opportunities for discussion occur naturally, never brush them aside just because they weren't in your original lesson plan. Always try to find some time for them if you possibly can.

Apart from these spontaneous discussions, discussions are often specified in the **Student's Book**, as activities on which you should spend at least five and possibly as much as ten minutes.

To occupy this amount of time usefully, you will have to act as a good chairperson, asking supplementary questions to keep things going, and making sure that different points of view are contributed. Questions such as 'Does everyone agree with (Name)?' or 'Do you think the same as (Name) and (Name)?' or 'Has anyone a different opinion from (Name)?' or 'Surely you don't all agree with (Name)?' are the stock in trade of chairing a discussion. Sometimes it may be useful to let students put up their hands to see how many think one thing, and how many another.

Keep your own views secret until at least the end. Discussions are not a time for you to impose your 'orthodox' views on the class, but for students to have the excitement of working things out for themselves.

Speechmaking

Being able to make a good speech depends, like many other uses of language, on thorough preparation. Students are asked to undertake a *Factfinding mission* and collect facts which will be the basis of their speech. A week or so later they are given time to write this material up into speech form, and then reduce it to brief notes. The actual speeches (of about 60 seconds each) should be delivered with only these notes in the speaker's hand, or even without notes at all.

Role play

Role plays also require careful preparation. After forming the pairs or small groups required, each student should choose which part he or she is to play and (to increase spontaneity) shouldn't look at the other parts. Students may be able to choose their own parts, but a less time-consuming method is to share out the parts, either according to a pre-arranged plan you have made, or by drawing lots.

Students will need a few minutes to study their parts and think about things to say before speaking begins. The members of the group should then speak to each other in an impromptu way (no written notes), each trying to react appropriately to the things the others say. If they go off track, they may start again. You should meanwhile go from group to group, helping as necessary, but interfering as little as possible. When everyone has had plenty of practice (this may take as long as 15–20 minutes) choose one or two groups to perform in front of the class.

2.5 Focus on listening

Listening comprehension

For each of these, students choose from a range of answers to a set of comprehension questions. A full explanation of the task appears in the **Student's Book** and the script you have to read aloud can be found in **Appendix 2** of this book.

Introduce the task. Make sure students understand what they have to do. Tell them to lay down their pens while you read the script for the first time.

Read the script again. This time the class perform the task.
Let the class hear the script a third time, if you think necessary. Check the answer(s). Write the correct answer on the board so that students can correct their work.

Dictations
These are all of the unprepared type. The scripts are in the **Unit-by-unit teaching notes**.
Read the passage three times as follows:
1 continuously at a fairly low speed (students with pens down);
2 in short sections of a few words each, indicated by the line breaks (/). Repeat each section after a few seconds, before moving on to the next section. Students write during this stage;
3 continuously again, at normal speed.

After the third reading allow students two minutes to check their work before handing it in for correction. (See **Section 1.6** for suggestions on correction and marking.)

2.6   Focus on pronunciation

The majority of drills are concerned with stress in words of more than one syllable, stress in emphatic and contrastive sentences, and some basic intonation tunes. A few of the more difficult sounds are also practised.
Several different procedures are used. These are explained in the **Unit-by-unit teaching notes** and instructions in the **Student's Book**.

2.7   Focus on writing

Here are some guidelines for the Directed Writing Units:
- Ask students to read the question or instruction carefully and to identify:
  1 the purpose of the task;
  2 the audiencer/reader;
  3 the text type required.
- If the stimulus reading text has a title, ask students to study it and to predict the content.
- Ask student to skim read the text to confirm their predictions.
- Student work in pair/groups and read the text carefully, paying attention to the purpose of the task. The should write down any relevant points from the text.
- With the whole class, elicit points from each/group and write them on the board. Then still as a class, let student eliminate any irrelevant points and add any that have been omitted.

- Next, focus on the format of the text type to be produced. Discuss the style and tone of the piece of writing, making sure that it is relevant to the audience/reader.
- Students write a first draft.
- Ask student to work individually or in groups to edit their drafts, using these question to guide them:
  1. Has all the relevant content been included?
  2. Does the writing suit the pirpose of the task?
  3. Does the piece of writing address the appropriate reader?
  4. Does the writing convince the reader of the writer's point of view?
  5. What about the organisation of the content? The grammar? The punctuation? The spelling?
  6. Has the writer kept to the stipulated number of paragraphs?
  7. Has the writer respected the word limit?

This method of working will train students to work in three stages:
- self-questioning and making notes;
- making a plan and sorting the notes according to the plan;
- writing a draft in full sentences.

For the continuation beyond the draft stage, see **Section 1.6** on correction and marking.

2.8 Integrating literature

The National Syllabus emphasises the importance of the link between language and literature. Most of the reading passages are taken from contemporary literature. Both African and non-African writers are represented, though the former predominate.

Among the questions which follow reading texts there are often one or two which relate to the style and literary quality of the passage, rather than the interpretation of facts in it – that is some questions are concerned with appreciation rather than comprehension. The two types of questions are not usually separated from each other or distinguished in any way, as we wish students to get used to the idea of evaluating as well as understanding while they read.

There is, in addition, a place for short stories which can be read for enjoyment only, and not turned into formal work by the addition of lots of questions and exercises. Texts of this kind should be read for the pleasure they give. They are best read silently in class, when students can ask you questions about any points they cannot work out for themselves. They can be read at any point when you think five or ten minutes of silent reading will be beneficial, e.g. after a demanding oral activity, such as a role play.

3 Unit-by-unit teaching notes

UNIT **1**

1a In pairs or groups, students discuss the questions. Then open up the discussion to the whole class. Elicit the answers to the questions. Students may not know that the Commonwealth began over four hundred years ago with the first English settlements in North America. The Commonwealth is now a voluntary organisation of autonomous states which were formerly possessed by the British Empire. The organisation is fairly informal and it allows heads of Commonwealth countries to meet at frequent intervals to discuss common problems and co-operation. It has no rules which members must obey. It is based on a common history which covers the colonial period and many of the countries have similar education systems. English is the common language of the organisation. The British monarch (king or queen) has always been the head of the Commonwealth and it is run by a Commonwealth Secretariat. Cameroon joined the Commonwealth in 1995.

1b Read the instructions with the class. Students read the text silently. Then read the text aloud. Read parts yourself and ask individual students to read the rest. Clarify any difficult vocabulary as you proceed, e.g. **sanctions** (punishment), **objective** (aim), **transition** (change).

In pairs or groups, students discuss and list the challenges Chief Emeka faced and the achievements he recorded. Ask individuals to read a point from their list.

2a Follow Procedure 2.7. Students draft their report. Correct the drafts and return them to students to make a fair copy. These writing tasks can be done for homework.

2b In groups, students discuss the questions. Then open up the discussion to the whole class.

3 Answers:
1 -ee   2 It usually means a person.   3 The verb.   4 Absentee does not fit the pattern because it is based on the adjective. Amputee does not fit the pattern because it is based on the shortened verb.   5 A person who is interviewed   6 C – trainee

4
Follow Procedure 2.5 for *Listening comprehension*. The script is in **Appendix 2**. Read the script without pausing while students listen. Give students time to read the questions silently. Read the script again, pausing for students to circle the correct answers. Read the script a third time to let students check their answers.

Answers:
1 D   2 C   3 A   4 D   5 B   6 A   7 D   8 C   9 B   10 B

5
Give students a choice of speaking for or against the motion. Then give them a few minutes to make notes about what they wish to say, either for or against the motion. Hold a class debate, taking speakers alternatively for and against the motion.

6
Tell students to read the reading text again silently. They then make a plan of their essay. Ask one or two students to read out their plan. Write it in note form on the board. Students write their essay in draft form. Correct the drafts and return them to students to make a fair copy. The last two tasks can be done for homework.

7a
Select individuals to read the two sentences aloud. Ask students to discuss the questions in pairs. Then read the explanation with the class.

7b
Give students time to read the five pairs of sentences silently. Then select individuals to read a pair of sentences. Ask the class to identify the word which is stressed in each of the second sentences.

8a
Give students time to read the idioms and the definitions silently. Ask individuals to read the example sentence for each one. Then ask students to use the idiom in a new sentence.

8b
In pairs or groups, students decide how to complete each of the sentences. Select individuals to say a completed sentence.

16 UNIT-BY-UNIT TEACHING NOTES

Answers:
1 talk of the devil   2 is talking through her hat   3 talking nineteen to the dozen   4 the talk of the town   5 sweet-talked

9a Read the notes in the **Grammar Review Section 8.14** with the class.

9b Read the explanation and examples with the class.

9c Free answers.

9d Give students time to read **2.1–2.4** in the **Grammar Review Section**. Students then write out the passage, inserting the articles where necessary.

Answers:
1 The   2 0   3 the   4 0   5 the   6 a   7 a   8 an   9 the
10 the   11 0   12 the   13 0   14 the   15 the   16 0   17 a
18 0   19 0   20 0   21 0   22 the   23 a   24 the   25 the
26 the   27 the   28 a   29 a   30 a   31 a   32 the   33 the
34 an   35 an   36 an   37 the   38 the   39 a   40 the

10 Free answers. Give students time to discuss the proverbs. Then ask them for equivalent proverbs in their own or other languages.

11a Read the explanation with the class.

11b Say the sentences. Students repeat after you. In pairs, students then practise saying the sentences.

UNIT 2

1 In pairs, students discuss the questions. Then ask individuals the questions. Free answers.

2a Give students time to read the passage. Then read the passage with the class. Tell students to ask about any difficult words. The new words in colour are practised in **4**.

2b Students write the answers to the questions. This can be done for homework.

Answers:
1 F: He is a professor of psychiatry. **2** T **3** T **4** F: 15% remember physical discomfort, 50% remember emotional discomfort. **5** T

2c Check that students understand what a bar-chart is. Draw a simple example on the board. Students can then work in pairs to draw a bar-chart based on the information in the passage.

Answer:

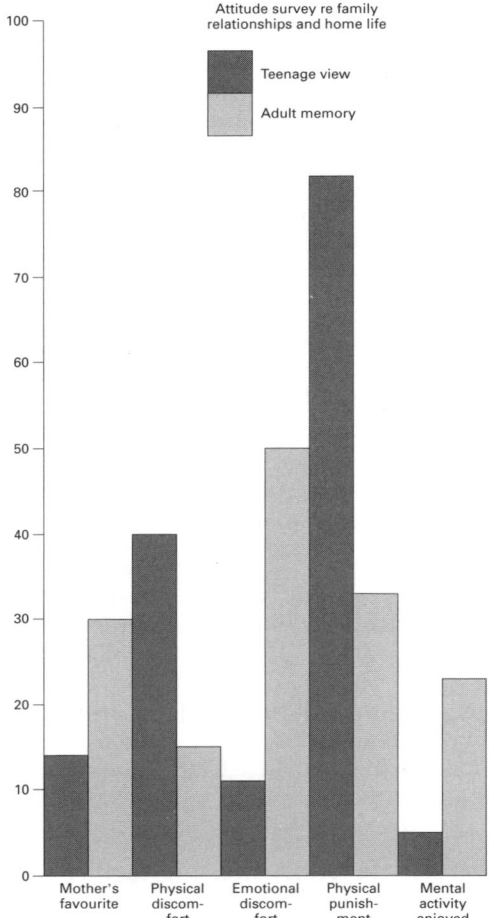

18 UNIT-BY-UNIT TEACHING NOTES

3a In groups, students talk about their favourite musicians and discuss the questions. Ask groups to report back to the class.

3b Students read the passage silently. Then read the passage with the class. Check any difficult vocabulary as you read, e.g. **controversy** (argument or disagreement), **spitting image** (to look exactly like someone), **ambience** (the way a place makes you feel), **strident** (too loud and high). The words in colour are practised in **4**.

3c Give students time to write the answers to the questions. Ask individuals the questions.

Answers:
1 Abeokuta in 1938. 2 Twenty-four. 3 One: Seun 4 His father and his younger brother, Seun. 5 Sixteen. 6 His father didn't agree at first. He advised him to leave school and to study music full time. 7 From watching his father play. 8 No, he draws inspiration from American music and the African way of life. 9 The people, his friends talking, parties, waking up in the morning, hearing the birds, the cars, everything about African life. 10 He's pragmatic, open-minded and cool-headed.

4 In pairs, students use dictionaries to check the meaning of the adjectives from the two passages they have read. Give them time to compose a sentence for each adjective, then ask individuals to read a sentence.

5a Read the idioms and definitions with the class. Ask students to use each idiom in a new sentence.

5b In pairs or groups, students decide how to complete the sentences. Select individuals to read a completed sentence.

Answers:
1 like a man 2 a man of his word 3 hitting a man when he's down 4 my own man 5 every man for himself 6 man to man 7 a man of the world 8 the man in the street 9 to a man 10 man and boy

6 These topics relate to family life, and the material in the reading passages in **1** and **3**. Students follow the instructions and complete the task.

7a Read the explanation and examples with the class.

7b Say the sentences. Students repeat after you. Students then practise the dialogues in pairs. Select pairs to read a dialogue.

7c Students write the dialogues with arrows to indicate the rise-fall tone.

   Answers:
   1 A: The plane lands at Sacred Heart College to ↘ night.
      B: At Sacred Heart ↘ Col ↗ lege?
      A: Yes, at Sacred Heart ↗ Col ↘ lege.
   2 A: Alice Amin came last in the 100 metres ↘ race.
      B: She ↘ came ↗ last?
      A: Yes, she ↗ came ↘ last.

7d Students create dialogues in pairs. Ask different pairs to read their dialogues. Free answers.

8a Read the explanation and examples with the class.

8b **Free answers such as**:
   1 ..., not having to get up and go to work. 2 ..., turning the water to silver. 3 ..., submerging the houses. 4 ..., dreaming of their future life together. 5 ..., thinking how silly the words were.

9 This task should be done for homework. Students find out as much as they can about the Kora award, and musicians who have won it. Students can then report back to the class. Open up the discussion to the whole class.

10a Students choose one of their favourite musicians, as discussed in **3**. They should make notes about the musicians's career, and then write a draft. Correct the drafts and return them to students to make a fair copy. The writing tasks can be done for homework. Select a few individuals to read their account to the class. You could make a list on the board of the most favourite musicians in the class.

10b Ask students to read the interview in 'Here comes the Son' again. In groups, students talk about what questions they could ask a musician, and what answers they might receive. Make sure they use direct speech. Make a list of questions and answers on the board. In pairs, students can then write a draft of their interview. Correct the drafts and return to students to make a fair copy. The writing task can be done for homework. Select a few pairs to read their interview.

UNIT 3

1a Students discuss the questions in pairs or groups. Then ask individuals the questions. Free answers.

1b Before reading about the tasks, give students time to read the whole article silently. Go through the article with students, asking them to define any difficult vocabulary, e.g. **culinary** (connected with cooking), **vile** (evil/very bad), **fungal** (adjective applied to mushrooms, e.g. fungal growth), **exotic** (very unusual), **dank** (dark and damp), **mycophiles** (mushroom lovers), **edible** (eatable), **species** (kinds), **insouciance** (carelessness), **exhort** (urge), **heed** (take notice of). Check they can define all the words printed in colour, as they will be using these in **3b**. Read the instructions describing the tasks students will carry out. Students read the article again, making notes for the tasks.

2a In groups, students discuss the uses of fungi and make notes for their exam answer. With the help of students, draw up a plan for the exam answer on the board. Students draft their exam answer. Correct the drafts and return them to students to write a fair copy. The writing tasks can be done for homework.

2b In groups, students make a list of modern threats to fungi. As a class, discuss the style of writing required for a newspaper article. With the help of students, draw up a plan for the article on the board. Students draft their article. Correct the drafts and return them to the students to make a fair copy. The writing tasks can be done for homework.

3a **Answers:**
All the words in colour are adjectives. *Appetising* is a present participle; *contaminated* is a past participle.

3b Free answers. Students write their own sentences using the words. Ask individuals to read one of their sentences.

4a In pairs, students read the advertisement and compile a list of possible questions, e.g. Which African countries do they deliver to? How do they transport the documents and packages? By plane? By truck? By train? How much do they charge for documents and packages? How long does it take for a parcel from Cameroon to reach South Africa? How frequent is the service? Students also think of possible answers.

4b Read the instructions for the role play. Students carry out the task.

5a Ask students how a formal business letter differs from an informal letter. List the standard openings and endings for the two kinds of letter on the board.

5b Students prepare a plan of their letter. Ask individuals to read one step from their plan. With the help of students write an agreed plan on the board. Students draft their letter. Correct the drafts and return them to students to write a fair copy. The writing steps can be done as homework.

6a Read the explanation and examples with the class.

6b Give students time to prepare the sentences. Select individuals to read a modified sentence.

A guide to answers:
1 When/Because he struck out in another direction, Uchendi Nwani changed his life. 2 As/When it stretches out its fingers, the baby can touch various parts of its body. 3 As Narcissus sat peacefully by the pool of water, he did not know that he was growing roots into the ground. 4 When she discovered that her son was wanted by the police, Uchendi Nwani's mother advised him to give himself up. 5 Parents may affect their children's emotional development if/when they give them away for adoption. 6 Because/When/As I learnt that there were other people in the world, I began to love them. 7 When Oedipus killed his father and married his mother, he did not realise they were his parents. 8 My parents were kind and understanding, as/because they helped me to pass through the difficult teenage years intact.

22 UNIT-BY-UNIT TEACHING NOTES

7 In groups, students discuss the picture and think of possible story lines for their composition. Open up the discussion to the whole class and make notes of an agreed plan on the board. Students write a draft. Correct the drafts and return them to students to write a fair copy. The writing tasks can be done as homework.

UNIT 4

1 In pairs or groups, students discuss the questions. Ask a few individuals the questions. Free answers.

2a Students read the passage silently. Then read it with them, identifying any difficult vocabulary, e.g. **trudge** (slow walk), **sprawling** (widespread), **irony** (sarcasm), **unseemly** (unpleasant), **forage** (search), **infrastructure** (roads, etc.), **galling** (upsetting/annoying), **propriety** (legality), **ostensibly** (apparently), **reluctant** (unwilling), **stakeholders** (people with an interest in something), **seamier side** (nastier side).

2b In pairs, students read the questions and decide on the answers. Ask individuals the questions.

Answers:
1 They walk to work because bus fares would cost most of their earnings.   **2** Free answers, e.g. slum; shack; less than $1 a day; piles of stinking refuse; dressed in rags.   **3 a** The walkers are too miserable to appreciate the beauty of the dawn rising over the national park.   **b** budding/beginning to grow   **c** The number of poor people is growing while the rest of the economy is shrinking.   **4** Free answers, e.g. many people are poor; many people live in slums; wages are low; most workers are casual labourers; Kenya is the 22nd poorest country in the world; GNP of $280; enrolment in schools is falling; there is no rubbish collection; the infrastructure is in disrepair.   **5** Free answers, e.g. mismanagement by official bodies; government corruption.   **6** Free answers.   **7** Free answers.

3a Students read the second passage silently. Check understanding of difficult vocabulary, e.g. **thriving** (prosperous), **vulnerable**

UNIT-BY-UNIT TEACHING NOTES 23

(defenceless), **fluctuating** (changing), **stagnated** (remained unchanged), **rehabilitate** (repair).

3b In pairs, students prepare answers to the questions. Ask individuals the questions.

A guide to answers:
1 The once prosperous copper industry has collapsed. People who once got free housing, education and medical care are now living in poverty.   2 (a) In places like Ndola, many stores have closed down and most people live in compounds or shanty towns. Unemployment is about 80 per cent in places like Nkwazi compound. (b) Unemployment and crime rates are high. The cities are empty. People have lost access to free medical care and education and now live in shanty towns.   3 The crisis is forcing people to rely on themselves.   4 The writer thinks Zambia has a future because he says it is rich in human and natural resources.

4 Give students time to read the passages again and prepare answers to the questions.

A guide to answers:
1 The crisis in Kenya is the result of mismanagement and corruption. The problem in Zambia is that the country was dependent on one industry: copper. When the copper price collapsed, the economy collapsed with it. The situation was made worse by mismanagement of the industry.   2 The people in both countries have realised that they cannot rely on the government to help them. As a result, Kenyans have started small businesses. In Zambia, the poor are setting up their own schools to educate their children. There are many such community-based projects.

5 Read the questions with the class and take answers from individuals.

Answer:
Meaning 7.

6 This task should be done for homework. Students decide on a country they would like to visit and find out more about it. They then prepare a speech about the country, to be given in step 10.

7 Follow Procedure 2.4 for **Role play**. Read the instructions for the role play with the class. In closed pairs, students prepare and practise their roles. Select a few pairs to act their roles for the class.

8a Read the idioms and definitions with the class. Ask students to use each idiom in a new sentence.

8b In pairs or groups, students decide how to complete the sentences. Select individuals to read a completed sentence.

Answers:
1 was given the cold shoulder   2 poured/threw cold water on
3 blow hot and cold   4 leaves them cold   5 cold comfort
6 made my blood run cold   7 getting/having cold feet

9 Follow Procedure 2.5 for *Listening comprehension*. Read the script in **Appendix 2** without pausing while students listen. Give students time to read the questions. Read the script again, pausing for students to circle correct answers. Read the script a third time, without pausing, to allow students to check their answers.

Answers:
1 B   2 A   3 D   4 C   5 C

10 Select a few students to deliver the speech they prepared in step 6.

UNIT 5

1a In pairs or groups, students discuss the questions. Ask individuals the questions. Free answers.

1b Read the instruction with the class. Students read the article silently. Tell students to ask about any vocabulary they do not understand. Ask students for the meaning of: **albino** (lacking in colour), **stereotype** (false picture), **prejudice** (feeling against).

2a Follow Procedure 2.7. Students prepare their talk. They select relevant points from the checklist.

UNIT-BY-UNIT TEACHING NOTES 25

2b Read the instruction with the class. Students then write their talk. This can be done for homework.

3a Read the explanation and examples with the class.

3b In pairs, students practise saying the sentences with the correct intonation. Select individuals to say a sentence.

4a Read the pre-reading question with the class.

4b Students write out the passage using the correct verb forms.

Answers:
1 shaded 2 stretching 3 was reflected 4 ran 5 murmuring 6 spent 7 enjoying 8 walked 9 would stop 10 would sit 11 talk 12 wanted 13 told 14 was 15 talked 16 had learnt 17 had never seen 18 bubbled 19 did 20 chatted/were chatting 21 gathered 22 filling 23 were following 24 saw 25 fill 26 winked 27 asked 28 thought 29 was 30 made 31 jump 32 shouted 33 clapped 34 heard/had heard 35 disappeared 36 went on 37 walking 38 talking 39 had ever seen

Ask the pre-reading question. Free answers.

5a Read the idioms and definitions with the class.

5b This task can be done orally. Give students time to prepare the sentences. Then select individuals to say a completed sentence.

Answers:
1 don't have the heart 2 had our hearts in our mouths 3 do we know by heart 4 broke his heart 5 has a heart of gold 6 have set my heart on 7 after their own heart 8 have had a change of heart 9 to pour out her heart 10 will eat my heart out

6 Follow Procedure 2.7. In pairs or groups, students discuss what it is like to be the odd one out. They note down ideas for their essay. Students draft their essay. Correct the drafts and return them to students to write out a fair copy. The writing tasks can be done for homework.

26 UNIT-BY-UNIT TEACHING NOTES

7a Working in pairs, students give the talk they prepared in step 2.

7b Pairs discuss the questions.

7c Pairs discuss the questions. When students have had enough time for discussion, select an individual to give their talk to the whole class, who then analyse and criticise the talk constructively, i.e. Was the tone friendly? Were the points clearly expressed? Was the language suitable for oral delivery? Then, as a class, discuss the differences in writing to be read silently and writing for reading aloud.

Practice Test 1

This part of the Practice Test follows the format of the reading comprehension activities in the Understanding and Response Units, and is intended as exam practice for the Understanding and Response paper in the GCE O'level exam. Before students start, remind them of the guidelines for doing reading comprehension (see Procedure 2.3) and suggest they spend at least twenty minutes at the start of the exam, reading both passages carefully. Let the class try the paper under exam conditions. Time them (40 minutes) so that they get used to working within a time limit. Take the papers in and mark them yourself. There are 7 answers. Mark the content of answers 1–6 out of 5 each and the content of answer 7 out of 10, giving a total of 40 for content. Allocate 30 marks for overall language accuracy. Go through the answers in the next lesson.

1 **Answers:**
Passage 1
1 Her success was like a fairytale because it was almost unbelievable. She started with nothing except a good idea and her culinary skills and built up her business to include four factories, 1,100 workers with a turnover of GB£100 million. 2 She started in her kitchen at home with six staff and sold her products to neighbourhood takeaways. The business grew and within six months it had moved to a local industrial estate. Supermarkets began to buy her products, allowing her to open more factories and take on more staff. 3 Perween's husband gave up his career as a medical doctor to work full time in the business as the marketing manager. Her sons, on the other hand, have no interest in working for the company and are pursuing

UNIT-BY-UNIT TEACHING NOTES 27

their own careers in London: one is setting up his own business and the other works for British Telecom.

Passage 2
4 Helen loved growing up in the quiet, orderly atmosphere of the village. She liked the traditional customs, beliefs and family life of the village. When she moved to the city to join her mother, she was unhappy and confused. Life in the city was harsh, women were treated badly and it seemed an un-African way of life.   **5** She believes the African woman's role is to protect her children from bad influences. She also believes in traditional African family roles regarding women and is critical of un-African ways of living.   **6** She started by painting realistic pictures. She then began to put her feelings about the conflict between traditional and modern ways into her pictures. She conveyed the contrast between rural and urban life and consequently the people in her pictures became distorted.

Both passages
7 There is really no comparison between the difficulties faced by the two women. Perween came from a comfortable professional family where she was supported from the age of 16 by her doctor husband. The only problem she had was fitting in her commercial activities with looking after her family. However, she did face the challenge of succeeding in a predominantly white, male business world. Helen, on the other hand came from a very poor background. She developed her art in spite of having to survive in the harsh environment of the city. She succeeded by working hard, winning a competition and finding a good teacher to help her.

2 This part of the Practice Test follows the usual format for **Listening comprehension**. However, the task should be completed under exam conditions, within a time limit (30 minutes). Read the script in **Appendix 2** without pausing while students listen. Give students time to read the questions. Read the script again, pausing for students to circle correct answers. Read the text a third time to allow students to check their answers. Take the papers in and mark them yourself. There are 6 answers. Allocate 5 marks for each answer, giving a total of 30 marks. This gives a total of 100 for Practice Test 1. Go through the answers in the next lesson.

Answers:
1 C   2 C   3 A   4 D   5 B   6 B

UNIT 6

1 In pairs, students discuss the questions. Then ask individuals the questions. Free answers.

2a Students read the passage silently. Then read it with the class. Clarify any difficult vocabulary, e.g. **receptor** (receiver), **sour** (opposite of sweet), **dubbed** (named), **paediatric** (relating to children), **taste bud** (part of tongue which tastes things), **speculates** (guesses), **sweet tooth** (liking for sweet things), **tantalising** (teasing).

2b In pairs, students read the questions and decide on the answers. Ask individuals the questions.

Answers:
1 Taste receptors: a pair of proteins that snake in and out of cells in our tongue. 2 They are a recent discovery. The scientists responsible for the discovery are still doing research on how taste receptors function. 3 There are five: sweet, bitter, sour, salty and umami. 4 A sense of taste evolved because man needed to know which foods were good (sweet) and which were bad (bitter). Bitter foods are often poisonous. 5 They wanted to find the gene that produces a protein which acts as a taste receptor. 6 They discovered one gene which produces a protein they called TR1. They used this to find similar genes and discovered a protein which they called TR2. Each receptor is linked to a taste region of the tongue: TR1 with sweet areas and TR2 with bitter ones. 7 They could be used to find a drug to block the bitter receptor and allow children to take bitter medicines without complaining.

3a Give students time to read the passage silently. Then read it with the class. Identify any difficult vocabulary, e.g. **subtle** (hard to recognise), **significantly** (much), **exacerbating** (making worse), **osteoporosis** (weakening of the bones), **concede** (admit), **herbivores** (vegetable eaters), **insipid** (weak).

3b Answers:
1 They fed him solid food too early and gave him too much salt.
2 Both studied the effect of different levels of salt intake on blood pressure. 3 Lower blood pressure and fewer deaths

UNIT-BY-UNIT TEACHING NOTES 29

among older people from stroke. **4** Excessive salt intake can lead to higher blood pressure and result in heart attack and stroke; it can exacerbate osteoporosis; it is indicated in stomach cancer. **5** They are exposed to more salt than adults because snack foods are aimed at children and, because of their higher metabolic rates, they take in more food per gram of body weight than adults. **6** Addiction began 10,000 years ago when man became a farmer and adopted a diet low in meat and high in low-salt plants. To preserve meat, salt was used and man became addicted to salty foods. **7** The food industry puts a lot of salt in processed foods to give flavour to tasteless ingredients; salt retains water and makes the foods weigh more to produce more profit; people buy more drinks when they eat salty snacks.

4 Give students time to read both passages again and to decide on answers to the questions. Then ask individuals the questions.

A guide to answers:
1 The authors of both texts are preoccupied by the biological consequences of taste preferences. **2** Both texts explain that humans evolved a sense of taste as a guide to a suitable diet, e.g. humans need salt and crave it when they have too little.

5a Read the explanations and examples with the class.

5b Give students time to prepare the sentences. Then ask individuals to say a completed sentence.

Answers:
1 Raised **2** Adjusting **3** wishing **4** stacked **5** taken
6 dancing **7** caught **8** panting **9** fearing **10** broken

5c Free answers.

6a Read the idioms and definitions with the class. Ask students to use each idiom in a new sentence.

6b In pairs or groups, students decide how to complete the sentences. Select individuals to read a completed sentence.

Answers:
1 get our tongue round **2** to keep a civil tongue **3** found her tongue **4** on the tip of my tongue **5** bitten her tongue off **6** hold your tongue **7** a slip of the tongue

30 UNIT-BY-UNIT TEACHING NOTES

7a In pairs, students discuss the question. Ask individuals the question.

7b Students complete the tables.

Answers:

art	**artistic**
individual	**individualistic**
realism	realistic
geometry	geometric
symbol	**symbolic**
style	**stylistic**
imagination	**imaginative**
decoration	**decorative**
communication	**communicative**
representation	**representative**
creation	**creative**

7c Select individuals to read a noun-adjective pair.

8 Follow Procedure 2.4 for **Role play**. Read the instruction. In pairs, students practise the roles. Then select a few pairs to act their roles for the whole class.

9a Read the explanation and answers with the class.

9b In pairs or groups, students take turns to say a sentence using the rise-fall tone for the question tags. Select individuals to say a sentence.

9c Repeat the procedure, this time for the fall-rise tone.

10 Read the instructions with the class. Students draft an account of their role play. Correct the drafts and return them to students to make a fair copy. The writing tasks can be done for homework.

UNIT 7

1a In pairs or groups, students discuss the statements. Ask individuals whether they agree or disagree with each statement. If they disagree, they should correct the statement. Free answers.

1b Students copy the statements into their exercise book, correcting any that they think are false as they do so.

A guide to corrected answers:
1 Science is not solely for boys. **2** Girls do not do better than boys in science. **3** Students do not perform badly in science because science is difficult. **7** Teachers should not always lecture the students in science lessons. **8** A good science teacher is not one who only has a knowledge of scientific facts. **10** A good science teacher moves from the simple to the complex.

1c Read the instruction. Give students time to read the text silently. Then read the text with the class. Check comprehension of any difficult vocabulary, e.g. **transmission style** (teacher talking and students listening), **regurgitate** (throw up without digesting), **adherence** (sticking to), **liturgy** (religious ceremony), **acquisition** (learning), **facilitate** (make easy).

1d In pairs, students discuss the questions. Then ask individuals the questions.

A guide to answers:
1 The author does not quote any experimental findings in support of his/her argument. This is the main weakness of the article. **2** It must have been the 'transmission style' the author criticises so vehemently. **3** It would have helped if the author had produced some statistics or at least some examples from personal experience to support his arguments.

2a Follow Procedure 2.7. Read the instructions. Students write a draft of their talk. Correct the drafts and return them to students to make fair copies. The writing tasks can be done for homework.

2b Read the instructions. Students write their paper following the same procedure as in **2a**.

2c Read the instructions. Students write their letter following the same procedure as in **2a**.

3 This task can be done for homework over the period of a week. Students write up their report in preparation for giving their talk in step 8.

4a Read the words to the class and ask individuals to say them after you.

4b Repeat the procedure as in **4a**.

5 Read the instructions. In pairs or groups, students discuss the question. Ask individuals to report their opinion to the class.

Free answers, such as:
(clockwise from top left) You shouldn't have any complaints, but if you do they should be small complaints; don't bring anyone else with you to see the doctor; don't all try to get on the bus at once; please take your shoes off.

6 Follow Procedure 2.5 for **Listening comprehension**. Read the whole script in **Appendix 2**, without pausing, while students listen. Read each question from the script, pausing for students to write the number of the question and the correct letter in their exercise book.

Answers:
1 A   2 C   3 A   4 B   5 A   6 B   7 C

7 Follow Procedure 2.7. Read the instructions and expressions with the class. Students draft their letter. Correct the drafts and return them to students to make a fair copy. Select a few students to read their letter to the class.

8 In groups, students take turns to deliver the report they prepared in step 3. Compare answers as a class.

9 Follow Procedure 2.5 for **Dictation**, using this script:
The excitement of science

UNIT-BY-UNIT TEACHING NOTES 33

We live surrounded / by the apparatus of science: / the diesel engine and the experiment, / the bottle of aspirins and the survey of opinion. / We are hardly conscious of them; / but behind them we are becoming conscious / of a new importance in science. / We are coming to understand / that science is not a haphazard collection / of manufacturing techniques / carried out by a race of laboratory dwellers / with acid-yellow fingers and steel-rimmed spectacles / and no home life. / Science, we are growing aware, / is a method and a force of its own, / which has its own meaning and style / and its own sense of excitement.

UNIT 8

1 In pairs or groups, students discuss the questions. Ask individuals the questions.

Free answers, such as:
1 I smoke because I enjoy it / my friends smoke. I don't smoke because it is unhealthy / I can't afford cigarettes. **2** People smoke because they find it relaxing / they think it is sophisticated / their friends smoke / they are addicted to nicotine. **3** It is unhealthy. It affects / annoys other people who do not smoke. It is expensive. It is an addiction. **4** In developed countries, non-smokers are very intolerant of smokers. The situation in developing countries is different and smoking is tolerated much more.

2a Give students time to read the passage silently. Then read it with the class. Check comprehension of any difficult vocabulary, e.g. **warrants** (deserves), **obliterate** (destroy), **intolerance** (unwillingness to put up with something), **wantonly** (without reason), **rhetoric** (speech or writing used to persuade or influence people), **alleviate** (lessen), **indignation** (anger), **bravado** (daring), **myopia** (short-sightedness), **relinquished** (given up).

2b Give students time to read the questions and prepare answers. Then ask individuals for their opinions.

A guide to answers:
1 Smoking is definitely a public health problem. The cost of treating smoking-related diseases is enormous and places a

burden on the state.   **2** Smoking does warrant some public measures and not necessarily modest ones. For example, control of advertising which uses glamorous images to tempt young people into the addiction is necessary.   **3** The author is wrong. The fact that an addictive substance is sold for profit and then leads to a drain on public health resources is immoral.   **4** It is a fact, but it does not justify the sale of tobacco, since all the author is saying is that less than half of smokers die from their addiction.   **5** The author's main concern seems to be with the individual's right to a private life, but one gets the impression that he is really trying to justify the tobacco industry's right to profit from a dangerous drug.

2c Read the dictionary extract with the class. Then ask the question.

Answer:
Definition 2: not large in quantity, size, value, etc.

3a Give students time to read the passage. Then read it with the class, clarifying any difficult vocabulary, e.g. **prematurely** (early), **chronic** (incurable), **unfazed** (not put off), **implicating** (involving), **uncanny** (strange and difficult to explain).

3b Give students time to prepare answers to the questions. Then ask individuals the questions.

Answers:
1 The figure is an estimate based on large-scale studies.   **2** Because such a large number of unnecessary early deaths is very bad news.   **3** Smoking makes chronic diseases, e.g. respiratory diseases, worse and leads to early death in such patients.   **4** Peto found that tobacco makes a particular disease much more common which makes it an important cause of deaths from that disease.   **5** It does not mean that no deaths should be attributed to smoking. Other pollutants can cause cancer but smoking adds a pollutant which can hasten death from a particular disease.   **6** Heavy indoor pollution in colder cities in China is a contributing factor to lung cancer. This means that more non-smokers get lung cancer in China than in the West.   **7** Tobacco companies know that smoking kills, but they are always keen to show that other pollutants can cause diseases such as lung cancer.

4 Give students time to read both passages again silently and then ask individuals the question.

UNIT-BY-UNIT TEACHING NOTES 35

A guide to the answer:
The author of the first passage is keen to argue against legislation discouraging tobacco use. He plays down the statistics showing the relation between tobacco and premature death. He stresses the right of individuals to do what they wish. The second author exaggerates the serious nature of the problems associated with smoking. The situation is serious, but it is sometimes counter-productive to overstate the seriousness of a problem. This is shown by the failure of very aggressive anti-smoking campaigns which lead to more young people taking up the habit.

5a Give students time to read **Grammar Review Section 8.15**. They then decide on the correct tenses in the sentences. Ask individuals to read a corrected sentence.

Answers:
1 takes (present simple) 2 made (past simple) 3 play (present simple with future meaning) 4 have collected (present perfect) 5 retired (past simple) 6 has come (present perfect) 7 crashed (past simple) 8 escaped (past simple) 9 comes (present simple with future meaning) 10 was awarded (past simple passive)

5b Select one or two pairs to read the dialogue. Then give students time to prepare the report of the conversation. Select individuals to read a completed sentence.

Answer:
1 had heard 2 that day 3 had forgotten 4 her 5 the night before 6 his 7 had 8 his 9 him 10 their 11 had been 12 had 13 the next day 14 they 15 would 16 there

6 Read the explanation and examples with the class. Students then write down the antonyms for the adjectives in the list. Select individuals to read the completed pairs.

Answers:
1 unfair 2 illogical 3 inappropriate 4 impolite 5 ungovernable 6 inedible 7 irreligious 8 unpopular 9 irreplaceable 10 illiterate 11 insecure 12 imperfect 13 irrelevant 14 illegible 15 immoral 16 incurable

7a Follow Procedure 2.5 for *Listening comprehension*. The script is in **Appendix 2**. Follow the instructions in the **Student's Book**.

Answers:
1 C   2 A   3 C   4 B   5 B   6 A   7 C   8 C

7b In groups, students discuss the questions. Then ask individuals for their opinions.

8 Follow Procedure 2.4 for **Role play**. In pairs, students practise the role plays. Select pairs to act one of the situations for the class.

9 Follow Procedure 2.7. Read the instructions with the class. Discuss the aspects of smoking and drinking with them. Ask students for their opinions. Students then draft their essay. Correct the drafts and return them to students to make a fair copy. The writing tasks can be done for homework. Select one or two students to read their completed essay to the class.

UNIT 9

1a In pairs or groups, students discuss the questions. Ask individuals the questions. Free answers.

1b Read the three questions with the class. Students read the passage silently and look for the answers to the questions. Ask individuals the questions.

A guide to answers:
1 (1) Carnegie believed the rich should use their wealth to do good.   (2) Rosenwald believed that helping poor people to prosper was good for the people and also good for business.   (3) Norris believed that through education you can help people to help themselves.   **2** The demands on government are greater than the resources they can get from the private sector. Social problems can only be solved if the solutions can create new capital to provide further resources.   **3** Thanks to modern information technology, the most important human resource has changed from mechanical skills to knowledge.

UNIT-BY-UNIT TEACHING NOTES 37

Read the passage again with the class. Check comprehension of difficult vocabulary, e.g. **initiate** (begin), **bankrupt** (unable to pay debts), **innovator** (inventor of new ideas), **credo** (belief), **philanthropic** (charitable), **entrepreneur** (businessman/woman), **organic** (living).

1c Ask the question.

Answer:
Meaning 1.

2 Follow Procedure 2.7. In groups, students discuss the task and combine to make notes for their speech. Students draft their speech. Correct the drafts and hand them back for students to make a fair copy. The writing tasks can be done for homework.

3a Give students time to read the letters silently. Then ask students to tell the story in their own words. Select individuals to read the letters to the class.

3b Ask the questions.

Answers:
1 He must have ordered the book by letter. If he had called at the bookshop, he would have seen his wife. **2** He took care of minor medical problems on the expedition. **3** To record plant species in the rainforests of Mount Cameroon. **4** The second book, about restoring antiques has got nothing to do with his work in the rainforest. He is thinking of starting a business after he returns from Africa. **5** If Smith had not received the book, he may not have continued the correspondence and may never have seen his wife again. **6** They are the same person (Alison). **7** They had both changed their names. **8** He has given up his old life as a businessman who could only live in a city. He now appreciates the countryside and a quiet life. **9** Because the couple were about to be reunited at the airport.

3c Give students time to match the expressions. Ask individuals to say a pair of expressions.

Answers:
1 d **2** j **3** k **4** b **5** l **6** a **7** i **8** e **9** c **10** g **11** f **12** h

38 UNIT-BY-UNIT TEACHING NOTES

4 Follow Procedure 2.4 for **Role play**. Read the instructions. In groups, students prepare and practise their roles. Select one or two groups to act their roles for the class.

5 In the absence of a real Customs or Immigration officer, the teacher can prepare a talk about one of the jobs. Students make notes and then write up a summary of the talk.

6a In pairs or groups, students discuss the questions. Then open up the discussion to the class.

Answers:
1 Free answers. 2 The change in the relationship is reflected in the way the letters change from formal business letters to become informal, friendly and finally intimate.

6b Read the instruction. Give students time to work out the meaning of the idioms. Ask individuals to express the idioms in a simple form, e.g. the middle of summer; healthy; thinking about; mention; living in the countryside; is seen; write to me; stop corresponding; helps to avoid.

6c Give students time to prepare the sentences. Ask individuals to say a completed sentence.

A guide to answers:
… saves me from making mistakes. / … saves me from having a long walk. / … saves me from getting into trouble with the teacher. / … saves me from making mistakes. / … saves me from getting them dirty. / … saves me from making notes in class.

7a Read the explanation and example with the class.

7b Read the explanation and example with the class.

7c Students complete the chart in their exercise book. Select individuals to read a sentence and say whether the *-ing* form is an adjective, a noun or a verb.

Answers:
1 verb 2 noun 3 adjective 4 noun 5 verb 6 verb
7 verb 8 adjective 9 noun 10 adjective 11 verb
12 noun 13 verb 14 adjective 15 noun

7d Students review modal verbs. Read **Grammar Review Section 7.10** with the class. Read the instruction. Students choose ten sentences from the letters and classify them. This can be done for homework. Select individuals to read one of their sentences and to classify the modal.

8 Free answers.

9 In pairs or groups, students practise saying the sentences. Select individuals to say a sentence.

10 Follow Procedure 2.7. In groups, students think of possible continuations for the story and make notes. They then draft their story. Correct the drafts and return them to students to make a fair copy. The writing tasks can be done for homework. Select a few individuals to read their story to the class.

UNIT 10

1 In pairs or groups, students discuss the questions. Then ask individuals the questions. Free answers.

2a Students read the passage silently. Then read the passage with the class. Check comprehension of difficult words, e.g. **staple** (basic), **phenomenon** (feature), **obligations** (duties), **utilised** (used), **ultimately** (finally), **recompense** (payment). The words in colour are dealt with in **2c**.

2b Give students time to prepare answers to the questions and then ask individuals the questions.

Answers:
1 The main difference is that women today often organise themselves into clubs and self-help groups. **2** Historically, their main focus was to organise and conduct joint festivities, but they also provided mutual help for the members of the group. **3** Joint farming of fields / establishment of savings and loan

schemes / cooperative shops / group operation of mills / cooperative livestock farming.   **4** Free answers.

2c In pairs, students discuss the expressions. Then ask individuals what they mean.

2d Students make a table showing the verb, the adjective and the antonym, adding five more examples of their own. Ask individuals to read out a set from their table.

Answers:
1 recognise   recognisable   unrecognisable   **2** account   accountable   unaccountable   **3** afford   affordable   unaffordable   **4** accept   acceptable   unacceptable   **5** admire   admirable   not admirable

3a Give students time to read the passage silently. Then read the passage with the class. Check comprehension of any difficult vocabulary, e.g. **pivotal** (important), **impetus** (forward movement), **categorical** (specific), **initiatives** (ideas), **disintegrated** (fell apart).

3b Give students time to prepare answers to the questions. Ask individuals the questions.

Answers:
1 In pre-colonial times, women formed self-help groups within their communities. In the 1950s, clubs were formed to familiarise women with western ideas on housekeeping and agriculture. After independence the clubs started to disintegrate but were revived by the government in the 1970s.   **2** A typical group now has 25 to 30 members and a management committee consisting of a leader, a secretary, a treasurer and five additional members.   **3** The fact that the women can themselves dispose of the money earned through the group. The income from the individual farm is usually controlled by the husband.   **4** Apart from agriculture, the groups undertake small projects such as trading, craft-work and savings schemes.

4   Give students time to read both passages again silently. In pairs or groups, they discuss the answers to the questions. Ask individuals the questions.

1 The main concern of the groups in both passages is to improve the economic status of women so that they can care for and

UNIT-BY-UNIT TEACHING NOTES 41

educate their children. **2** They have allowed them to become more independent of men; to run their own small enterprises; and to have money of their own to take care of themselves and their families. **3** Self-help groups tackle small projects and are generally quite successful. State-led groups on the other hand try to tackle large, ambitious projects which generally fail because they do not get sufficient technical support from the state. **4** Society benefits because the women raise their standard of living through their own efforts, which allows them to bring up healthy, educated children. **5** Free answers.

5a Students read the section in *WORD Magazine* on pages 140–141 of the **Students' Book**.

5b In groups, students discuss the inventions and vote for a winner. The whole class then votes for a winner.

5c Ask individuals what they would add to the list and why.

6a Read the list with the class and ask the questions.

Answers:
The Agenda comes first. / It decides the order of items to be discussed. / It influences the order of topics in the Minutes. / The secretary writes the Minutes. / He/She writes them during the Meeting. / Taking dictation and doing listening comprehension tasks.

6b Follow Procedure 2.7. Read the instructions with the class. In groups, students prepare the Agenda for the Meeting. Then students prepare imaginary Minutes of the Meeting. When they have finished, ask them to compare their Minutes in their groups.

7 Read the instructions with the class. This task can be done for homework. Select a few students to make a report on their findings to the class.

8a Students read the comic strip.

8b Follow Procedure 2.7. Students imagine they take the mask to the museum and ask the curator if it is an antique. They write the story in draft. Correct the drafts and hand them back for the students to write a fair copy. The writing tasks can be done for homework.

9 Follow Procedure 2.5 for **Dictation**, using this script:
Traditional knowledge and skills
People will always have / usual or preferential access / to different types / of technical knowledge. / There are no 'rules': / in some places women are potters / and in others men. / In some places women tend animals, / and in others men do this. / Women and men may both / engage in farming, / but may use different methods, / produce different crops / or farm for different reasons. / The perceptions / that each sex has of technology, / and their expectations from it, / are formed within the technical knowledge / that they have / and the processes / with which they are familiar. / It may be necessary / to ask questions / about which kinds of knowledge / are considered more important, / how different kinds / of knowledge interrelate, / and how different technical concepts / may be transferred / to other areas / of technical activity. / The amount of work entailed / by the different roles and responsibilities / of men and women / will encourage or constrain / access to the use of technology, / through overall time availability / and the patterns of time use.

Practice Test 2

Both the writing tasks should be done under exam conditions within a time limit. Allow 40 minutes for the Directed writing and 30 minutes for the Picture composition. At the end of the Test, take the papers in and mark them yourself. Allocate 40 marks for content and 20 marks for language accuracy to the Directed writing. Allocate 25 marks for content and 15 marks for language accuracy to the Picture composition. This gives a total of 100 marks for Practice Test 2 Give individual feedback in the next lesson.

1 Students read the instructions and write the letter.

2 Students write a composition suggested by the picture.

UNIT 11

1a In pairs or groups, students discuss the questions. Ask individuals the questions. Free answers. Music piracy is a huge problem. It deprives artists and record companies of their return for their efforts. The pirated cassettes and CDs are often of inferior quality. The situation is also complicated by the exchange of recorded music through the Internet.

1b Read the instructions with the class. Students read the passage silently. Then read it with the class. Check comprehension of any difficult vocabulary, e.g. **bolster** (support), **counterfeit** (forged/illegal), **piracy** (theft), **rife** (widespread), **legitimate** (legal), **jeopardised** (harmed), **spectrum** (range), **plummeted** (dropped quickly), **bootlegger** (seller of fake goods), **indiscriminate** (random).

2a In pairs or groups, students discuss the points in the table and decide which ones a musician, who is losing his royalties, would use in a letter to the Ministry of Trade and Industry. With the help of students, compile a list of relevant points on the board. (Write numbers 1–12 on the board; tick relevant numbers and cross out irrelevant ones.)

2b Students write their letter using the layout suggested on page 97. The writing task can be done for homework.

3 Read the three statements with the class. In pairs, students discuss the statements and decide whether Fotabong is guilty of theft or not.

4a Read the instructions with the class. Ask students for their opinions. What do they think really happened? The evidence of the clerk who saw Fotabong counting only a small bundle of notes, and the bank manager who said the notes did not match the numbers of the notes supplied by the bank, points to the boss being the thief; he had the key to the safe.

4b Read the instructions and the plan for a formal report with the class. Take a class vote on who is the guilty party. Then ask students to supply the information which will go into the report. Students can make notes if they wish. Students can write the report for homework.

5a Read the idioms and definitions with the class. Ask students to use each idiom in a new sentence.

5b In pairs or groups, students decide how to complete the sentences. Then select individuals to read a completed sentence.

Answers:
1 worth her weight in gold   2 pulls her weight   3 throwing his weight about   4 a weight off her mind   5 to take the weight off my feet   6 to throw their weight behind it

6a Read the explanation and example with the class.

6b Say the sentences. Select individuals to repeat the sentences.

7a Read the explanation and examples with the class. Ask students to give further examples of nouns with Latin prefixes; write them on the board.

7b Give students time to try to work out the meanings of the words. Ask individuals to define the words.

7c Students write sentences using the words. Select individuals to read one of their sentences.

7d Students read the item on Latin prefixes in *WORD Magazine* on page 144 of the **Student's Book**. They write five more sentences. Select individuals to read one of their sentences.

8 Students read **Grammar Review Section 8.15** and then write the correct form of the verbs. Select individuals to read a completed sentence.

Answers:
1 came   2 holding   3 had made   4 threatened   5 told
6 was taking   7 managed   8 rang   9 had surrounded
10 were leaving   11 shouted   12 have surrounded   13 are covering   14 cannot   15 throw   16 will not harm

17 thought 18 could 19 will hold 20 run 21 broke
22 had not gone 23 shot 24 had happened 25 gave

9a Read the instructions and expressions with the class. In pairs, students write and then practise a dialogue using at least five of the expressions. Select pairs to act their dialogue for the class.

9b Read **Grammar Review Section 7.14** with the class.

UNIT 12

1 In pairs or groups, students discuss the questions. Then ask individuals the questions. Free answers.

2a Give students time to read the passage silently. Then read the passage with the class. Check comprehension of any difficult vocabulary. The words in colour are dealt with in **2c**.

2b Give students time to prepare answers to the questions. Ask individuals the questions.

Answers:
1 It comes from the Kiswahili word meaning 'brain'. **2** The population of the city is growing very quickly. Jobs are few and the poor need to use their brains and ingenuity to survive. **3** (1) Boys help motorists to find a parking place and guard the car for a small fee. (2) Paying a bribe to get preferential treatment at hospitals. (3) Men who tout for customers for vegetable sellers and then get a small reward when they bring a customer in. **4** One advantage is that it provides a small amount of money for very poor people who would otherwise go hungry. **5** He regards it as an attempt to justify the methods which sustain corruption. **6** (1) Real employment is hard to find. (2) Public employees are underpaid and need to make a little extra money by granting favours. (3) Getting official documents such as a passport, is a lengthy expensive business. Paying a corrupt official makes the task easy. **7** There's no money left long before the end of the month. Free answers. **8** These are metaphors. More examples: bursting at the seams (para. 2) /

charging the earth (para. 3) / creaking (para. 5) / snaking (para. 5) / the battle for the basket (para. 7) / turn yellow pages green with envy (para. 8) / corruption will be rooted out (last para.)

2c Students match the words with their meanings. Select individuals to say a word and its meaning.

Answers:
1 c 2 d 3 a 4 b 5 f 6 i 7 h 8 g 9 j 10 e

3 Read the instructions. In pairs or groups, students discuss the questions. Ask individuals the questions. Free answers.

4a Read the first part of the story with the class. It is important not to let students read ahead. Ask interim question 1. Free answers.
Repeat the procedure for the remaining parts of the story. Then give students time to read the whole story silently.

4b Give students time to prepare answers to the questions. Ask individuals the questions.

Answers:
1 The cyclist and his friends are all confidence tricksters. Their method is to gain the victims' trust by letting them win money in a three-card game. Their intention is to steal the victims' money later. The two peasants use a different method: they pretend to be simple-minded and to have a large sum of money with them. They pretend to be fooled by the city tricksters. They then wait for their chance to escape with the money they were allowed to win in the three-card game. 2 All the statements made by the men are lies. The two peasants only tell the truth when they are on their way back to their village. Free answers.
3 He is used to spotting victims for his confidence tricks.
4 At the beginning of the story, the pair look like typical unsophisticated country people. They behave as if they are not used to the big city and appear to be lost and unsure of themselves. At the end of the story they show themselves to be very sophisticated confidence tricksters who are full of confidence and self-assurance. 5 The man with the bicycle explained his plan to lure the victims into a false sense of security by letting them win at the three-card game. 6 The story is probably set in colonial times when the pound was the currency in use. The style of dress of the bicycle man, with two-tone shoes and white cork helmet also points to the colonial period. 7 ... it was firmly buckled, giving the impression that it contained some-

thing of value. It was important as bait to attract the attention of confidence tricksters.

4c Give students time to decide what the expressions mean. Ask individuals to explain them.

Answers:
1 something one often sees   2 they seemed to be   3 they were careful not to bump into people   4 the traffic was heavy   5 a crowd of people moving in all directions   6 Okeke didn't speak in answer to a question, he just shook his head   7 the man intended to cheat them   8 he shuffled the cards   9 he believed he was going to be rich

5 Follow Procedure 2.4 for **Role play**. Read the instructions. In pairs, students discuss the conversation that the confidence tricksters might have had and then role play it.

6 Students write their dialogue. Select pairs to act their dialogue for the class.

7 Follow Procedure 2.7. Read the instruction. In groups, students discuss the task and make notes for their essay. Students write a draft. Correct the drafts and return them to students to make a fair copy. The writing tasks can be done for homework.

8 Follow Procedure 2.5 for **Listening comprehension**. The script is in **Appendix 2**. Follow the instructions in the **Student's Book**.

Answers:
1 C   2 B   3 A   4 A   5 B   6 B

9a Read the explanations and examples with the class.

9b Students write three examples of their own. Select individuals to read one of their sentences.

10a Read the idioms and definitions with the class. Ask students to use each idiom in a new sentence.

10b In pairs or groups, students decide how to complete the sentences. Then select individuals to read a completed sentence.

Answers:
1 like nobody's business **2** had no business **3** means business **4** is none of your business **5** to get down to business **6** monkey business **7** minded my own business

UNIT 13

1a In pairs or groups, students answer the questions. Ask individuals the questions.

Answers:
1 (a) paediatrician (b) oculist (c) ophthalmologist **2** A surgeon. **3** Free answer. **4** Free answer. **5** Because you may get worse and die if you don't seek professional help. **6** Because it may not be suitable for the use to which you wish to put it. **7** Because they may swallow it and make themselves ill or die.

1b Give students time to read the text silently. Read the text again with the class. Check comprehension of any difficult vocabulary, e.g. **incapable** (unable), **unlicensed** (not approved officially), **untenable** (cannot be kept), **extrapolating** (calculating), **detoxify** (clear out poisons), **reluctant** (unwilling), **lucrative** (profitable), **patents** (registered ownership), **pharmacology** (medicines).

2 Follow Procedure 2.7. Read the instruction with the class. In pairs or groups, students discuss the points that they should put in their letter and make notes. With the help of students, draw up a plan for the letter on the board. Students draft their letter. Correct the drafts and return them to students to make a fair copy. The writing tasks can be done for homework.

3 Follow Procedure 2.5 for *Listening comprehension*. The script is in **Appendix 2**.

Answers:
1 She married a Gambian doctor and went to live in the country with him. **2** She worked in Nigerian teaching hospitals for some years. **3** An eye doctor. **4** B **5** E **6** False. **7** Both parents are doctors.

4 Read the instruction with the class. Students read the passage and circle the correct words in the list.

Answers:
1 D   2 A   3 B   4 C   5 E   6 D   7 A   8 E   9 D   10 C
11 B   12 A   13 E   14 D   15 D   16 A   17 C   18 D
19 B   20 A

5 Working in groups of six, students follow the procedure set out in Unit 2, step 6.

6 Follow Procedure 2.7. In groups, students discuss possible ideas for an essay prompted by the picture. With the help of students, draw up a plan for the essay on the board. Students draft their essay. Correct the drafts and return them to students to write a fair copy. The writing tasks can be done for homework.

UNIT 14

1 In pairs or groups, students discuss the questions. Ask individuals the questions. Free answers.

2a Students read the passage silently. Then read the passage with the class. Check comprehension of any difficult vocabulary. The words in colour are dealt with in **4c**.

2b Give students time to prepare answers to the questions. Ask individuals the questions.

Answers:
1 There are fewer fish in the lake and the size of the catch is getting smaller.   2 Three: Kenya, Uganda and Tanzania.   3 It was probably thought to be a good fish for fishermen to catch. 4 Because the Nile perch is a predator which has eaten all but two species of fish.   5 There are growing populations and industries around the lake. Mercury comes from the gold mines. Soap and cosmetics factories and chemicals from farms also pollute the lake.   6 It means that many fish are killed off, and sometimes the fish which survive are contaminated with toxins which, in turn, can harm people who eat them.   7 It began its

colonisation around the source of the Nile in Jinja at the Owen Falls Dam.   **8** It can be used to make paper, furniture and fertiliser.   **9** The seeds can survive for 30 to 35 years.   **10** The adjective 'fishy' is used to describe something which is suspicious or possibly illegal. In this case it is used to describe the fishing industry thus providing a good title for the passage.

2c Give students time to match the expressions. Then ask individuals to read out matched pairs.

Answers:
1 i   2 f   3 c   4 j   5 d   6 a   7 b   8 g   9 h   10 e

3 In pairs or groups, students discuss the questions. Ask individuals the questions. Free answers.

4a Give students time to read the passage silently. Then read the passage with the class. Check comprehension of any difficult vocabulary. The words in colour are dealt with in **4c**.

4b Give students time to prepare the questions. Then ask individuals the questions.

Answers:
1 Pesticides, herbicides, fertilisers, factory waste, household waste, dead trees, dead plants, ships, oil-tankers, nuclear accidents, sewage, livestock waste, bad roads, car emissions, burning wood and by-products of crops.   **2** Three: air, land and water pollution.   **3** Free answers.   **4** It built 450 sewage treatment plants.   **5** Emissions from factories and cars; gases from rotting vegetation; gases from livestock waste; gases from rotting household waste; the use of firewood.   **6** Many people are illiterate and are not aware that the things they do are causing gases which pollute the air.   **7** Most pollution comes from man's activities. The more people there are, the more pollution is caused.

4c Give students time to match the expressions. Select individuals to read a matched pair.

Answers:
1 g   2 a   3 f   4 b   5 h   6 c   7 d   8 e

5 Give students time to read both passages again silently. In pairs or groups, students discuss the passages, comparing them in

UNIT-BY-UNIT TEACHING NOTES 51

content and style. Free answers. Both passages deal with pollution; the first concentrating on the effect of water pollution on the fishing industry, the second dealing with all types of pollution. The first passage also considers the impact of over-fishing on the fishing industry. The style of the first passage is more informal then the second, which is in the formal, scientific register.

6 Follow Procedure 2.5 for *Listening comprehension*. The script is in **Appendix 2**.

Answers:
1 A   2 D   3 C   4 A   5 B   6 D   7 C   8 B   9 C   10 A

7a Students read the Calendar in *WORD Magazine* on pages 142–143 of the **Student's Book**.

7b In groups, students discuss the questions. Then open up the discussion to the whole class.

Answers:
(a) air pollution: burning of farm lands, hoeing and raking, harvesting, threshing.
(b) water pollution: land clearing; applying fertilisers.

8 Read the instructions. This task should be done as homework. Students prepare a short talk on their findings.

9 In groups, students take turns to deliver their talk. They then vote for the person in the group who gave the best talk. The winner from each group can then address the class. Finally, the class can vote for the overall winner.

10 In groups, students make an anti-pollution poster. It can be a collage of slogans and pictures. Posters informing students what they can do to protect the local environment could be used for a classroom display.

UNIT 15

1a In pairs or groups, students discuss the questions. Then ask individuals the questions. Free answers.

52 UNIT-BY-UNIT TEACHING NOTES

1b Read the instructions with the class. Give students time to read the article silently. Then read the article with the class. Check comprehension of any difficult words, e.g. **resurgence** (reappearance), **eradicated** (got rid of), **endemic** (permanently established), **parasite** (bug which lives off someone or something), **transmission** (passing on), **demise** (death), **eliminated** (got rid of), **vectors** (carriers).

2 Follow Procedure 2.7. Read the instructions for the task again with the class. Students draft their article. Correct the drafts and return them to students to make a fair copy. The writing tasks can be done for homework. (Note: Luxembourg, Corsica, Bulgaria and parts of Turkey are situated in Europe. Tajikistan, Azerbaijan, Armenia and Turkmenistan are situated in Asia.)

3a In pairs, students do the quiz. Ask individuals the questions.

Answers:
1 C   2 B   3 A   4 B   5 B   6 C   7 1:B   2:A   3:D   4:C
8 C

3b Read the questions and statements with the class. Ask the questions. Ask students to say whether they agree with the statement of opinion.

Answers:
Questions 1 and 3 are statements of fact. Question 2 is a statement of opinion.

3c Ask the question.

Answer:
It is possible to write an article on the importance of clean drinking water in maintaining a healthy body.

4a/b/c This task can be done for homework over the period of a week. In order to prepare for the task, read through the steps with the class. Have a class discussion about water-borne diseases, what causes them, what effect they have on people, how to cure them and how to prevent them in the first place.

5a Read the explanation and examples with the class.

5b Give students time to pick out the agent, action and object in the sentences.

Answers:
1 agent – action – object   2 object – action – agent   3 agent – action – object   4 object – action – agent   5 object – action – agent

Then read the note with students.

5c In pairs, students complete the dialogues. Select pairs to read a completed dialogue.

Answers:
1 It was brought by the foreign travellers.   2 It was alerted by the chief medical officer.   3 They were paid for by the tax-payers.   4 They were sung by primary-school children.   5 It was cured by modern medicines.

5d Read the instructions with the class. Give students time to prepare the sentences. Then ask individuals to read a sentence.

Answers:
1 Daniel was crippled by polio at the age of eleven.   2 Some steps were made by the village masons.   3 A meeting was called by the health worker.   4 The blind boy was led to school by Musa.   5 Emmanuel was made ill by over-eating.

6 Follow Procedure 2.5 for *Listening comprehension*. The script is in **Appendix 2**.

Answers:
1 Imaginary.   2 Atlantic Ocean.   3 Lagos/Sapele/Warri/Port Harcourt/Calabar   4 B   5 C   6 All the people will try and go to these buildings for shelter.   7 The Atlantic surged and caused flooding on May 24th, 1990.   8 An event that happens repeatedly, at regular times.   9 Global warming.   10 The ice-caps of the Artic region of the North pole and Antarctica in the south are gradually melting.

7 Students play the Dictionary Game in *WORD Magazine* on page 144 of the **Student's Book**.

54 UNIT-BY-UNIT TEACHING NOTES

8a Students circle the place names in the World Traveller Word Square in *WORD Magazine* on page 145 of the **Student's Book**.

8b Read the instructions. Students complete the task.

Answers:
Botswana: Gaborone
Brazil: Rio de Janeiro
Cameroon: Bafut, Bamenda, Buea, Douala, Kumba, Limbe, Mamfe, Tiko, Wum, Yaounde
China: Harbin
Congo: Kinshasa
England: Derby, London
Ethiopia, Addis Ababa
France: Paris
Ghana: Accra, Tamale
Kenya: Kisumu, Nairobi
Malaysia: Kuala Lumpur
Mozambique: Maputo
Nigeria: Enugu, Lagos, Port Harcourt, Sapele, Warri
Russia: Moscow, Ryazan
Sierra Leone: Freetown
Tanzania: Dar es Salaam
Uganda: Jinja
USA: Chicago, New York
Zambia: Kitwe, Lusaka, Ndola
Zimbabwe: Harare

Practice Test 3

1 Let the class try the paper under exam conditions within a time limit (40 minutes). Take the papers in and mark them yourself. There are 7 questions in Understanding and response. Allocate 5 marks to each question for content, giving a total of 35 for content. Allocate 20 marks for overall language accuracy, making a total of 55 marks for Understanding and response. Go through the answers in the next lesson.

Answers:
Passage 1
1 Most drugs administered to people and animals are excreted and released into the environment through sewage and farm waste. Up to 90 per cent of the drug administered is released in this way. It ends up in the purified water we drink. Little is known about the effects of these drugs on the environment

although we do know that they stop the growth of some plants and kill off some crustaceans. **2** Researchers have identified drugs in rivers and water supplies. An anti-chloresterol drug has been found in rivers in Germany and tap water in Berlin. The drinking water also contained antibiotics and anti-cancer drugs. In Florida, sedatives accumulated near a landfill where waste from a hospital was dumped. In the sea off Puerto Rico, drug residues seeped from millions of litres of pharmaceutical waste, dumped between 1972 and 1983. **3** Farm waste from animals is a major polluter of streams, rivers and reservoirs. Farmers use a lot of drugs to keep animals healthy and sometimes to promote growth. These are excreted and end up in water. Fish farmers put drugs in fish food. Up to 80 per cent of the drugs finish up beneath the fish cages.

Passage 2
4 Sulphur in the emissions from ships' smokestacks seeds clouds over the ocean. Water droplets condense around the sulphur particles. The clouds formed in this way reflect the sun's rays back into space and contribute to the reduction in global warming. **5** The calculation of the amount of sulphur emitted by ships was correct but it was assumed that it was emitted near the ports where the fuel was sold. In fact, it was spread over the oceans in long trails. **6** (a) Because ships travel over remote parts of the ocean emitting sulphur in the smoke from burning fuel. (b) Because they think that the cloud-generating effect is less in the cold northern hemisphere where most of the ships sail.

Both passages
7 Smoke emissions from ships may help in reducing global warming by generating clouds. Human excretions may be harming the environment because they contain drugs.

2 Students write the essay entitled 'Corruption', within a time limit of 30 minutes. Take the essays in and mark them yourself. Allocate 30 marks for content and 15 marks for overall language accuracy, giving a total of 45 marks. This will give a total of 100 for Practice Test 3. Give individual feedback in the next lesson.

Appendix 1

Contents analysis table

UNIT	Themes/Topics/ Type of writing/ Vocabulary development areas	Structures	Functions and skills	Spoken English	Important new words	
1	Public service The Commonwealth Interviews Essay writing Idioms: *talk* Proverbs	Conditional clauses without *if* Articles (revision)	Debating a motion	Fall-rise tone Contrastive stress (revision)	term of office advocate democracy sustainable suspend flout	sanctions promote negotiation consensus objective transition

2	Family life African music Idioms: *man* Essay writing – narrative and dialogue	Non-finite clauses	Making a speech	Rise-fall tone	rose-tinted psychiatric resonant physical conflicting subsequent	legendary implacable raucous meteoric pragmatic mean-spirited
3	Fungi and health Writing an exam answer Article writing Essay writing	More non-finite clauses	Asking for and giving information Writing a business letter (complaints)		culinary vile fungal exotic dank pallid avid mycophile edible species lethal insouciance exhort heed	appetising potent lurid irreparable nondescript toxic blameless patchy contaminated bulbous indispensable mutualistic intact

	Themes/Topics/ Types of writing/ Vocabulary development areas	Structures	Functions and skills	Spoken English	Important new words	
UNIT 4	Industry Economic crisis Social problems Town and country Geography Idioms: *cold*		Comparing and contrasting Persuading someone not to do something Making a speech		trudge sprawling irony unseemly forage infrastructure galling propriety ostensibly	reluctant stakeholders seamy side thriving vulnerable fluctuating stagnate rehabilitate
UNIT 5	Albinism Minority groups Writing a talk Essay writing – narrative Idioms: *heart*	Sequence of tenses (revision)	Describing people and things Giving a talk	Intonation	albino taunt pigment shun stereotype languish	recessive gene contagious prejudice discrimination genetic incestuous

6	Taste, food and health Idioms: *tongue* Keeping a diary	More non-finite clauses Word formation	Scientific description Communicating without words		receptor dubbed paediatric taste bud sweet tooth speculate tantalising	subtle significantly exacerbate osteoporosis concede herbivore insipid
7	Science education Teaching / learning styles Professional cooking Writing a talk Writing a conference paper Writing a letter of sympathy		Explaining a point of view Problem solving Expressing sympathy Giving an oral report	Fall-rise and rise-fall tones Stress Silent letters	strategies concepts preponderance transmission style regurgitate challenge predominate methodology qualification	involvement abstract unapproachable effervesce adherence liturgy acquisition facilitate consequently
8	Tobacco and health Teenage behaviour Essay writing – argumentative	Sequence of tenses (revision) Reporting speech (revision) Word formation	Giving explanations for behaviour Warning against smoking / drinking / drug taking Arguing a point of view		warrant obliterate intolerance wantonly rhetoric alleviate indignation bravado	myopia relinquish prematurely epidemic chronic unfazed implicate uncanny

UNIT	Themes/Topics/ Types of writing/ Vocabulary development areas	Structures	Functions and skills	Spoken English	Important new words	
9	Business The work of a customs officer Social responsibility Writing a speech Idioms and style Essay writing – narrative	More non-finite clauses -ing form (revision) Modal verbs (revision)	Requesting Asking for and giving explanations	Pronunciation – tongue-twisters	philanthropy philanthropic initiate bankrupt innovator	innovation credo entrepreneur organic resource
10	Women in society Agriculture Small enterprises Meetings Inventions Writing the Agenda and Minutes of a Meeting Essay writing – narrative		Describing and comparing		staple phenomenon obligations utilise ultimately recompense	pivotal impetus categorical initiatives disintegrate

11	Intellectual property Piracy in the music business Writing formal letters and reports Idioms: *weight*	Sequence of tenses Word formation – Latin prefixes	Refusing politely Problem solving	Intonation in reading lists	counterfeit bolster piracy rife legitimate	jeopardise spectrum plummet bootlegger indiscriminate
12	Corruption Confidence tricks and tricksters Writing a dialogue Essay writing Idioms: *business*	Verbs followed by *-ing*	Comparing and contrasting Making a plan		bumpkin creed decipher controversial wielding brandish lament	swindler haversack spotless reluctantly peer in anticipation
13	Drug safety and children Medical research Writing a letter to a newspaper Essay writing	Choosing the correct word	Impromptu speaking Describing		incapable unlicensed untenable extrapolate detoxify pharmaceutical	reluctant lucrative comprehensive patent pharmacology

	Themes/Topics/ Types of writing/ Vocabulary development areas	Structures	Functions and skills	Spoken English	Important new words	
U N I T 14	The fishing industry Pollution The environment Farming Making a poster		Comparing and contrasting Researching a topic (pollution) Giving a talk		undertake impact predator mercury eradicate persistent attribute to disillusioned scuffle contamination	cartel devastating undesirable combat pesticide herbicide sanitation injurious deterioration
15	Community health – malaria The spread of malaria across the world Water Human physiology Writing a magazine article Writing an information sheet	Active and passive The agent of an action	Persuading		resurgence endemic parasite transmission	demise resurgence eliminate vector

Appendix 2

Listening comprehension scripts
Unit 1, Step 4

Listen to a journalist talking about how he prepares to interview someone.

As a journalist, I have interviewed many sorts of people over the years. Some have had famous names – people whose life work has made them famous: politicians, writers, entertainers. Some have just jumped suddenly into the news, because of some chance occurrence: an eye-witness who saw a catastrophe, perhaps; or obscure men and women who are going to marry film stars, and are thus thrust unexpectedly into the limelight. As a result of all the interviews I have conducted, I think I can claim to have a few ideas about how to do a good interview. Here are some of the basic rules:
1. Research. Research is vital. Always find out as much as you can about the people you're going to interview, before you meet them. Try to understand the kind of work they do, or the life they lead. If the interviewee is a writer, read at least one of his or her books.
2. Preparation. Always prepare at least a few of your questions in advance. If, as in my case, the interview is the raw material for an article which is supposed to interest the general public, you need to have some preliminary idea what that article will be like. Is your aim to give a picture of the interviewee as a family man, concentrating on his character and the way he spends his leisure time at home? Or do you want him to tell you about his working career so far and his ambitions for the future? Try to think of yourself as a representative of the readers, and ask the sort of questions you think they would ask, were they conducting the interview instead of you.
3. Interest. Usually people won't let you interview them unless they trust you, so be sincere. If you write or phone to ask someone for an appointment, tell them why it's important (perhaps for both of you) that the interview should take place.
4. Atmosphere. The day of the interview arrives. You may be feeling nervous, but so may the other person. To be successful, an interview should be conducted in as relaxed an atmosphere as possible. Put the interviewee at ease with a few minutes of 'small talk' before you get down to the serious questioning.

Avoid embarrassing questions such as 'Was your mother married to your father when you were born?'
5 Accuracy and discretion. Don't rely on your memory. Make notes of any details you may want to quote in your article. If the best answers are very technical, it may be best to record them on a tape recorder. And be discreet, too, especially if the interviewee says something which sounds very controversial. Check that he really doesn't mind if the world knows what has just slipped out of his mouth, by asking, 'May I quote you on that?'

For example, you suggest to a government minister that officials have a very luxurious lifestyle, and he replies with a knowing laugh that they are all going to have their salaries cut by 10% next month, but don't know it yet; or you ask a television personality, 'Do you love your wife?' and the interviewee replies, 'I wish I'd never set eyes on her.' ('May I quote you on that?')
6 Integrity. The interview is over. All that remains is to write it up. But this is probably the most important part. You owe it to the person who gave you the interview to be fair. Let his words speak for him as much as possible. Every time you put an interpretation on his words, saying what you think he meant to say, there is a chance you will distort the facts.

Your reputation as an interviewer and reporter depends on observing these few simple rules.

Unit 4, Step 9

Listen to this article about the advantages of diesel engines.

That diesel engines have a longer life expectancy than their petrol equivalents is acknowledged. This is greatly enhanced by the introduction of anti-corrosion properties in diesel fuel, resulting in lower maintenance costs and a longer life of fuel systems. Detergents in the fuel help to keep the engine clean so that fuel injectors stay in tune and optimum performance is maintained for longer.

Diesel engines are also inherently safer than petrol engines due to the much lower flash point of diesel fuel. Diesel engines give more miles per litre as they operate with a large proportion of air to fuel, using approximately 20% less fuel than petrol engines. Their performance is made even better by the use of modern diesel fuels, which improve combustion.

Furthermore, a diesel engine emits approximately 1% of the level of carbon monoxide and 30% of the level of hydrocarbons of a petrol engine. So, diesel engines contribute significantly less

Practice Test 1, Step 2

Listen to this passage about Cheri Samba, an artist.

Cheri Samba, one of Congo's best-known painters, lives in Kinshasa. Now in his mid-thirties, Samba began as a commercial artist, illustrating newspapers and designing posters, advertisements and shop-signs. Influenced both by advertisements and comic strips, his paintings incorporate words – often in speech bubbles – in French or Lingala. The text provides a commentary on the images, giving voice to popular views and opinions. For example, his painting entitled 'The Big Market' depicts a bread thief being arrested at a crowded market. But the caption detailing the thief's wages and the cost of living reveals the social background of his 'crime' and the corruption of the soldiers who arrest him.

Samba's paintings are often parables or morality tales exposing social ills. Corruption is a frequent target, as in 'Professional Incompetence' where an official arranges an evening rendezvous with a female applicant. Elsewhere Samba criticises materialistic values. A painting of a woman surrounded by new furniture and electrical appliances is given meaning by its ironic title, 'Woman and Her First Desires'.

Samba's art responds to the changing social issues of the day and several of his recent paintings reflect on the threat of AIDS. In his painting entitled 'The Plague of the Century', a European and an African point accusing fingers at each other, quarrelling over whether AIDS began in Africa or in Western genetic experiments. Meanwhile, below them, both black and white skeleton-like figures die from the disease.

Unit 7, Step 6

1. How long can I keep your book before I return it?
2. It was very kind of you to lend me that book.
3. Do you know why the principal wants parents to give the school more money?
4. Shall we watch television after our evening meal?
5. The bulb has gone in the electric light in the kitchen and it's too high for me to reach, so I can't put a new one in.
6. Who does your hair for you in the morning?
7. Why on earth are you wearing that calabash?

(continued from previous: to 'smog' and 'acid rain'. And of course, diesel fuel does not contain lead, which is harmful to children's brains.)

Unit 8, Step 7

Listen to this passage to hear what happened when a mother found her three daughters smoking.

The other night I surprised my three daughters smoking in their bedroom. Everything about their manner showed that they were used to it: their way of holding the cigarette between their fingers and of raising it gracefully to their lips. Their nostrils quivered as they let out the smoke. And these young ladies did it behind the closed door, for I try as much as possible to respect their privacy.

The unexpectedness of it gave me a shock. The girls were surprised by my anger. A woman's mouth exhaling the acrid smell of tobacco instead of being fragrant! A woman's teeth blackened with tobacco instead of sparkling with whiteness!

I did not mind my children trying to keep up with the times. For example, I considered the wearing of trousers dreadful in view of our build, which is not that of slim Western women. But I gave in to that rush to fashion. Since my daughters wanted to be 'with it', I accepted the addition of trousers to their wardrobe.

But to grant themselves the right to smoke! Suddenly I became afraid of the flow of progress. Did the girls also drink? Who knows? One vice leads to another.

Was I to blame for giving my daughters a bit of liberty? My grandfather did not allow young people in his house. At ten o'clock at night, with a bell in his hand, he would warn visitors of the closure of the entrance gate. 'Whoever does not live here should scram,' he would say.

As for myself, I let my daughters go out from time to time. They went to the cinema without me. They received male and female friends. And the result is that under the influence of their circle of friends they have acquired the habit of smoking. And I was left in the dark.

I was aware of the harmful effects of tobacco, and I could not agree to its use. My conscience rejected it, as it rejected alcohol. From then on, relentlessly, I was on the look out for its odour.

Unit 12, Step 8

1 What shall I do? The police have arrested my brother, and he's innocent.
2 Will it be long before your father returns from America?
3 Why didn't your friend speak to you all the time you were dancing?
4 Did you find out how many cattle there were?
5 It's an honour to shake hands with you.
6 The bag you're holding looks very new.

Unit 13, Step 3

Listen to this passage about an opthalmologist in a million.

There is not much that can be said about eye care that Dr Hannah Faal does not know already. Until recently the only qualified opthalmologist in The Gambia, Dr Faal has spent the past ten years promoting eye health in a region where blindness lives side by side with poverty and ignorance. Her present work involves setting up eye care programmes as well as training hundreds of local personnel in the prevention of blindness and the care of the permanently blind.

In West Africa, a person has more than a one per cent chance of becoming blind, and there is only one opthalmologist for every million people. Yet much of the blindness could be prevented by a few simple precautions, and it is these that Dr Faal tries to teach to nurses in local hospitals and communities.

Dr Faal estimates that 80 per cent of eye diseases can be treated by persons who are not qualified as eye doctors, and that explains why she has been able to operate as the sole opthalmologist in The Gambia for so long. 'I train people to train,' she explains. She admits, however, that the task is a mammoth one and it will take many more years before the seeds of her work bear full fruit.

Born in Nigeria, in 1945, it was her marriage to a Gambian doctor that took Dr Faal to The Gambia. Now a mother of four children, her eldest child is also a medical student in Britain.

Dr Faal studied opthalmology at University College Hospital in Ibadan, in 1971, and then did a course at the Royal College of Surgeons in London, in 1975, before returning to Nigeria to practise in various teaching hospitals.

But it was not until she started working in The Gambia that Dr Faal encountered blindness in its early stages and realised the need for preventive medicine. The training she had received was inadequate for dealing with blindness and blinding diseases on the scale which she encountered in The Gambia. 'A lot of what I know I simply had to teach myself,' she says.

Unit 14, Step 6

Pronunciation note: *nkejje* = en-kedge-ee

Listen to this passage about nkejje fish in Lake Victoria.

For the people living along the shores of Lake Victoria in the Jinja District of Uganda, fishing has traditionally had a very important role in the economic, social and cultural aspects of their lives. Women make use of the fish which exist in this area of fresh water to ensure the livelihood of their families.

The nkejje is of particular importance for preventing malnutrition and related childhood diseases. This small fish, with an average size of three inches, contains 56.4% protein, 11% calcium and 8% fat.

Traditionally, women of Jinja have been involved not only in the processing of fish products, but also in fishing itself. Traditional fishing gear consisted of lift baskets, swim traps or scooping baskets. Women would weave this equipment out of papyrus, tree bark, banana fibres and creepers and use them in shallow waters for fishing.

As modern fishing technology has replaced traditional equipment, women's sphere of activity has become limited to the processing of the fish. The low fat content of the nkejje makes it suitable for sun-drying. Women prepare a clean rock on which they place the nkejje for sun-drying, cover with grass to preserve the flavour and also protect it against direct exposure to sunlight. The drying process continues at night due to the heat radiating from the rock surface.

Traditionally the nkejje fish is believed to be preventive against measles and kwashiorkor. For a child who already has measles, 'There is no better treatment,' says an old woman from Jinja. 'The nkejje is boiled and the child can drink the water and get better.' However the women of the Jinja District are now faced with a severe shortage of the nkejje fish.

The introduction, in 1965, of Nile perch and tilapia into Lake Victoria under a scheme supported by the Ugandan government and two international development agencies, has led to serious social, economic and ecological changes. The Nile perch fed on the nkejje almost to the point of making it extinct. While the commercial catch of the Nile perch increased from 0.24% in 1981 to 55% in 1985, that of nkejje fell from 96% in 1981 to none at all in 1985. Being dependent on the high-protein nkejje to combat malnutrition in their children, low-income mothers particularly have suffered from the scarcity of the fish.

Unit 15, Step 6

Global warming

It is a normal June day in Victoria Island, the fashionable Lagos district for those Nigerians who have money and influence. A threatening rainstorm early in the night keeps most of the suburb's residents indoors and its roads free of traffic. Suddenly, with no early warning system in place, the Atlantic Ocean lets loose its waters, hitting the beach with powerful high waves.

Within three hours, most of the island's properties are submerged in the roaring Atlantic, leaving the last few floors of high-rise buildings to play the part of a modern-day Noah's ark. As a presidential order commands the armed forces and the fire brigade to start on immediate rescue operations, news reaches Lagos that Sarone, Warn, Port Harcourt and Calabar, the nation's other port cities, have been swallowed by the rampaging ocean surge. Estimates put the casualties at two million dead and ₦100 million in damages to property, goods, factories and farms.

This gripping, science-fiction story is not far-fetched. On Thursday May 24th, 1990 the Atlantic, in what has become a periodic event, surged again. It threw panic and fear over the land as the Bar Beach, the nation's most popular beach, was reduced to a giant flood plain. Many buildings and roads, including Ahmadu Bello Way and Bishop Oluwole Street where 80 per cent of the state liaison houses in Lagos are, were mere frail reeds against the attack of the ocean.

What has gone wrong? Global warming, say the experts. According to them the world has grown warmer, particularly in the last decade. The great ice-caps of the Arctic region of the North Pole and Antarctica in the south are gradually melting and sending immense quantities of water into the seas. The result is a global swelling of sea levels, a development that pushes the excess of waters over the coastal regions of the world. Thus the climates of Nigeria, Canada's Tundra region and the Soviet Union's Siberia are inextricably linked together.

Appendix 3

Wordlist

This list includes the words, phrases and idioms printed in colour and actually practised in exercises. It also includes some other key vocabulary. The number after each entry is the Unit in which it appears in colour.

A
abnormal 11
acclimatise 9
adopt 2
advocate 1
after someone's heart 5
ailment 9
(*have an*) air (*about one*) 12
ambient atmosphere 14
anticipation 12
apparently 12
appetising 3
as man to man 2
assume 9
at heart 5
avid 3
avoid (*bodily contact*) 12

B
be about one's business 12
be in business 12
birth certificate 9
bite one's tongue off 6
blameless 3
(*make someone's*) blood (*run cold*) 4

bodily contact 12
break someone's heart 5
briskly 12
bulbous 3
(*rural*) bumpkin 12
burgeoning 4
(*be in*) business 12
(*get down to*) business 12
(*go/be about one's*) business 12
(*have no*) business 12
(*like nobody's*) business 12
(*make something one's*) business 12
(*mind one's own*) business 12
(*monkey*) business 12
(*be none of someone's*) business 12
(*send someone about his*) business 12

C
cartel 14
challenge 7
(*a*) changed man 9

(*a*) change of heart 5
(*cold as*) charity 4
circulate 11
circumstantial 11
(*blow hot and*) cold 4
(*out in the*) cold 4
cold as charity 4
cold as marble 4
cold comfort 4
(*get/have*) cold feet 4
(*get the*) cold shoulder 4
(*give someone the*) cold shoulder 4
(*in*) cold blood 4
(*leave*) cold 4
(*make someone's blood run*) cold 4
(*pour/throw*) cold water (*over/on*) 4
competence 9
concentration 13
contagious 5
contaminated 3
(*jump to a*) conclusion 9
confidence trickster 12
confiscate 12
conflicting 2

APPENDIX 3   71

consequently 7
contractor 12
controversial 12
counterfeit 11
(*essential*) creed 12
culinary 3
current trend 14
curse (n.) 5
cut (*a pack of cards*) 12
cyclostyling 12

D
dank 3
decipher 12
dehydration 15
demise 15
democracy 1
(*talk of the*) devil! 1
diarrhoea 15
dire straits 4
discharge 14
discrimination 5
divorce/divorced 9
dominant 14
(*talk the hind legs off a*) donkey 1

E
eat one's heart out 5
effervesce 7
embark on 14
embroidered 12
emission 14
enclose/enclosed 9
endemic 15
entrepreneur 2
epidemic 8
essential (*creed*) 12
every man for himself 2
evolution 6
exotic 3
expedition 9
expose 13
extrapolate 13

F
familiar (*sight*) 12
(*get/have cold*) feet 4
find one's tongue 6
firsthand knowledge 9
fluctuate 4

G
genetic (adj.) 5
get one's tongue round 6
get the cold shoulder 4
give someone the cold shoulder 4
give tongue 6
glance (n.) 4
go about one's business 12
go to bed a rich man 12
(*have a heart of*) gold 5
growth industry 4

H
hand over (v.) 14
hasty 9
(*talk through one's*) hat 1
have a heart of gold 5
have an air about one 12
have no business 12
have one's heart in one's mouth 5
have one's heart in the right place 5
haversack 12
(*talk one's*) head (*off*) 1
have the heart 5
(*after someone's own*) heart 5
(*at*) heart 5

(*break someone's*) heart 5
(*a*) change of heart 5
(eat one's) heart (*out*) 5
(*have a*) heart of gold 5
(*have one's*) heart (*in one's mouth*) 5
(*have one's*) heart (*in the right place*) 5
(*have the*) heart 5
(*know by*) heart 5
(*learn by*) heart 5
(*pour out one's*) heart 5
(*set one's*) heart (*on*) 5
(*take*) heart 5
hit a man when he's down 2
hold one's tongue 6
huge sums 14

I
immature 13
implacable 2
implement 10
impressed 12
incestuous 5
indigenous 13
indispensable 3
infrastructure 4
initiative 7
innovator 9
insipid 6
insist 9
intact 3
intolerance 8
investment 9
irreparable 3

J
jeopardise 11
jump to a conclusion 9

APPENDIX 3

K
keep a civil tongue 6
keep in touch 9
know by heart 5

L
learn by heart 5
leave cold 4
legendary 2
legitimate 11
lethal 3
life is not a walk in the park 2
like a man 2
like nobody's business 12
lurid 3
luxury 4

M
mainstay 10
make a man of someone 2
make someone's blood run cold 4
make something one's business 12
man and boy 2
(*the*) man in the street 2
(*a*) man of his word 2
(*a*) man of the world 2
(*as*) man to man 2
(*cold as*) marble 4
mean business 12
mean-spirited 2
metabolic rate 6
meteoric 2
methodology 7
migration 15
milling (*throng*) 12
mind one's own business 12
modest 8
money-go-round 10

monkey business 12
(*have one's heart in one's*) mouth 5
moral indignation 8
mutualistic 3
mutual support 10

N
nondescript 3

O
osteoporosis 6
outlook 9
(*one's*) own man 2

P
pallid 3
parastatals 12
patchy 3
peep in 12
peer in 12
pending 9
philanthropy 9
physical 2
piracy 14
population explosion 14
potent 3
pour cold water on 4
pour out one's heart 5
poverty 4
practised (*eyes*) 12
pragmatic 2
precaution 11
predator 14
predominate 7
premature 11
prematurely 8
preponderance 7
preserve 14
principally 7
principle 1
procure 10
promote 1
property 6
prosecution 9

psychiatric 2
pull one's weight 11
purification 14
put up with 9

Q
qualification 7

R
radical (adj.) 9
raucous 2
recessive gene 5
regurgitate 7
reluctant 12
remote 9
representational 3
resemblance 9
resist 12
resonant 2
resurgence 15
retrenchment 4
rhetoric 8
rife (adj.) 11
rose-tinted 2
run-off (n.) 14
rural (bumpkin) 12

S
saleable 10
sanitation 15
scuffle 14
(*prove one's*) self-worth 2
send someone about his business 8
set one's heart on something 5
(*a*) shake (*of one's head*) 12
(*talk*) shop 12
(*get the cold*) shoulder 4
(*give someone the cold*) shoulder 4
shred 14
(*a familiar*) sight 12
sight (v.) 14

(*someone's heart*)
  sinks 5
skin graft 11
(*a*) slip of the tongue
  6
small talk 1
solidarity group 10
sour-faced 12
spare (*oneself*) 4
split up 9
spotless 12
stand for (=
  represent) 9
(*too much of a*) strain
  9
stream of cars 12
submerge 11
subsequent 2
sub-standard 11
supernatural 11
supersonic 11
sweet talk 1
swindler 12

T
take a weight off
  someone's mind 9
take heart 5
take the weight off
  one's feet 11
(*small*) talk 1
(*sweet*) talk 1
talk the hind legs off
  a donkey 1
talk nineteen to the
  dozen 1

talk of the devil! 1
(*the*) talk of the town
  1
talk one's head off
  1
talk shop 1
talk though one's hat
  1
(*an easy*) target 7
taste receptor 6
taunt 5
term of office 1
throng 12
throw cold water on
  4
throw's one's weight
  about 11
throw one's weight
  behind 11
(*have on the*) tip of
  one's tongue 6
to a man 2
(*bite one's*) tongue
  (*off*) 6
(*find one's*) tongue
  6
(*get ones'*) tongue
  (*round*) 6
(*give*) tongue 6
(*have one's*) tongue
  in one's cheek 6
(*hold one's*) tongue
  6
(*keep a civil*) tongue
  6
tontine 10

toxic 3
tough (*roots*) 2
traditional 7
transmission 15
trick (n.) 12
trouble fund 10

U
unapproachable 7
unchecked 14
unsaleable 10

V
vigorous 12
vile 3
vital 12
volunteer (v.) 9

W
(*pull one's*) weight
  11
(*take a*) weight (*off
  someone's mind*)
  11
(*take the*) weight (*off
  one's feet*) 11
(*throw one's*) weight
  (*about*) 11
(*throw one's*) weight
  (*behind*) 11
wheeling and
  dealing 12
with one's tongue in
  one's cheek 6
worth (*one's/its*)
  weight in gold 11